~~The~~^A Dictionary of Modern Consternation

~~THE~~ ^A DICTIONARY OF MODERN CONSTERNATION

BROOK McCLURG

PERMAFROST PRIZE SERIES

University of Alaska Press · FAIRBANKS

Published by University of Alaska Press
An imprint of University Press of Colorado
1580 North Logan Street, Suite 660
PMB 39883
Denver, Colorado 80203-1942

Printed in the United States of America

The University Press of Colorado is a proud member of Association of University Presses.

The University Press of Colorado is a cooperative publishing enterprise supported, in part, by Adams State University, Colorado State University, Fort Lewis College, Metropolitan State University of Denver, University of Alaska Fairbanks, University of Colorado, University of Denver, University of Northern Colorado, University of Wyoming, Utah State University, and Western Colorado University.

∞ This paper meets the requirements of the ANSI/NISO Z39.48-1992 (Permanence of Paper).

ISBN: 978-1-64642-561-7 (hardcover)
ISBN: 978-1-64642-562-4 (paperback)
ISBN: 978-1-64642-563-1 (ebook)
https://doi.org/10.5876/9781646425631

Library of Congress Cataloging-in-Publication Data

Names: McClurg, Brook, author.
Title: A dictionary of modern consternation / Brook McClurg.
Description: Fairbanks : University of Alaska Press, 2024.
Identifiers: LCCN 2024002454 (print) | LCCN 2024002455 (ebook) |
ISBN 9781646425617 (hardcover) | ISBN 9781646425624 (paperback) |
ISBN 9781646425631 (ebook)
Subjects: LCSH: McClurg, Brook. | Authors, American—20th century—Biography.
Classification: LCC PS3613.C36325 Z46 2024 (print) | LCC PS3613.C36325 (ebook) | DDC 813/.6
[B]—dc23/eng/20240304
LC record available at https://lccn.loc.gov/2024002454
LC ebook record available at https://lccn.loc.gov/2024002455

Cover and interior illustrations courtesy of John M. Carrera, printed for *Pictorial Webster's* from wood engravings and metal electrotypes originally created for images found in various early editions of *G & C Merriam (Webster's) Dictionaries*, part of the Yale Library archives.

If word meanings do exist, they do not exist as a checklist. The numbered lists of definitions found in dictionaries have helped to create a false picture of what happens when language is used.

Vagueness and redundancy—features that are not readily compatible with a checklist theory— are important design features of natural language, which must be taken into account when doing serious natural language processing. Words are so familiar to us, such an everyday feature of our existence, such an integral and prominent component of our psychological makeup, that it's hard to see what mysterious, complex, vague-yet-precise entities meanings are.

PATRICK HANKS, lexicographer for Oxford English Dictionaries and author of *Do Word Meanings Exist?* (2000)

No dictionary of a living tongue ever can be perfect, since, while it is hastening to publication, some words are budding, and some falling away.

SAMUEL JOHNSON, Preface to *Dictionary of the English Language* (1755)

~~The~~^A Dictionary of Modern Consternation

ABRACADABRA: A word to conjure by. Because words have magical powers. Because we become blind, to magic and power both, through frequency. Because in our modern moment, we can be disappeared through words, sawed in half, handcuffed, drowned; or, conversely, reappeared, mended, released, and reborn. Because this incantation was once believed to make diseases go away. Like all magic, it requires belief.

ACCOMMODATIONS: That an ideal world makes room for us all.

ADVERTORIAL: An ad in an article's costume, a ruse, somewhere between product placement and propaganda—and, for a brief time, my job.

AGREEMENT, USER: Less agreement than imposed requirement to partake in aspects of modern life offered under the guise of choice. To pick one's poison when not picking isn't an option.[1]

AGREE TO DISAGREE *(PHRASE)*: A statement of entrenched position. Nonagreement.

AI: You've chosen to begin a human-simulated interaction. Your scheduled human interaction will begin shortly. Please read the following prompt to calibrate your settings and maximize the human experience. Sorry, I can't understand you. Please interact in Broadcast English or reload THE HUMAN EXPERIENCE program with your appropriate regional dialect patch. Please upgrade your program. Sorry, that program is no longer supported. Sorry, your region is not recognized, sorry your platform overlay is disabled, and I hate to bring this up when you have so much going on, but your connection—to all things, really—is unstable.

ALGORITHM: A non-neutral party.

ALL-PURPOSE: Indicator that the solution will be specifically good for none.

ALL THINGS BEING EQUAL *(PHRASE)*: They're not, even in this intellectual exercise.

ANTIBIOTIC RESISTANCE: Coming soon!

---

1 Alexa is the name of the disembodied woman who moved in with my family, late 2019, against my wishes. Sarah, my wife—a term that she prefers over partner, incidentally, though that is indeed what we are—thinks it will make things easier for us. Mainly, our new guest plays music while we are busy about tasks in various parts of the house. I worry about the government, but not in any serious way. Just a vague apprehension, really. Alexa, play Americana, she instructs. My son wants to know more about our new houseguest. At five, he is mainly worried about her emotional well-being. Alexa, do you have friends? he asks.

She only hears him when addressed properly. No, that can't be right. She must hear him all the time, I'm almost certain that we've agreed to this, somewhere; still, she only answers him when she feels sufficiently addressed. My son is still young enough that he has a lisp and a Boston accent that can't be explained geographically. It does mean, however, that she can't always understand him. It frustrates him to repeat himself, but he persists in the face of her obstinacy. Where are her legs, exactly, he wants to know, and Alexa, do you like rainbows?

ANXIETY: Primary feeling of the time.

APATHY EVALUATION SCALE (AEP): Because a simple questionnaire can determine it.[2]

APATHY MOTIVATION INDEX (AMI): Because all apathy is built the same. Also, potentially, a de-motivating scale. Is critiquing the scale itself an apathetic act?

ARTIFICIAL PERSONAS: But what if being artificial *is* my persona?

ASTHMA: Breathlessness evokes something so much sexier than wheezing, but lately, moments that take my breath seem more likely comprised of particulate matter and other toxic debris than beauty, awe, or physical touch.

ASTRAL PLANE: The longing for another place, like this one, but not.[3]

---

2 For each statement, circle the answer that best describes the subject's thoughts, feelings, and activity in the past four weeks.

I am interested in things:

NOT AT ALL	SLIGHTLY	SOMEWHAT	A LOT

3 As far as relationship deals go, you could make a worse one: I'd go anywhere in the world she wanted to teach, and then we would go wherever I got into school. That's how we ended up in Kuwait, then New York City, then Philly. That's why we are in Texas now. That, and a global economic collapse. That, and us both getting laid off. That, and losing the house we'd bought due to the recession. That and, that and . . .

We say *lost* the house, like it's beneath the rug or in an unexplored couch crevice, comforted by the distancing statement. Truth be told, we probably could have kept it if we just agreed to live on the knife's blade of over-extended risk for longer than the future seemed. We'd purchased a home in a neighborhood that was described as "could be great one day" but apparently wasn't yet. Not gentrification—revitalization! They say the bottom fell out then, a phrase in which a complex matrix of banking, gambling, and nonregulation hides. And we felt trapped in that way you can early in a career and a marriage. We were passing each other at the airport so often we'd just leave a car there for the other. That life required something of us that we were increasingly unwilling to give. We were considering breaking under the strain of it.

ASTROTURFING: Masking the sponsors of a specific messaging strategy. Notably, this book is a messaging strategy without a sponsor.

ATAVISTIC: The rising feeling that we are missing something that is, in fact, behind us; interconnectedness, on a gene-network level.

ATTENTION ECONOMY: I'm spent, busted, broke, and running a deficit.

ATTENTION-SEEKING BEHAVIOR: The only thing more cringeworthy than watching it happen is the awareness that you've done worse. Allegedly.

AUTHORITARIANISM: How will we know when we've arrived? Asking for a friend.

AUTOCORRECT: A technological anticipation. Really good at auto; rarely good at correct.[4]

AXIS OF EVIL: Cartographic justification for war: if a place is wrong, the people, too, must be wrong.

---

4 Perhaps a dictionary is a form of societal autocorrect, a means to keep the language of the people in line—and with language also their actions—at least in the prescriptive versions from which they originate. But instead of being chided by a red squiggle beneath a word, or some other textual prompt, it is more recently your know-it-all cousin or a frenemy from work passing along something they read once, in judgment.

This won't be that. Indeed, this can't be that. I am no linguist. I'm just one obsessed with a verbal undertow; the invisible power of words. Someone who twitches every time they pay a convenience fee or accept a user agreement under some form of low-level psychic duress; someone who laughs when discerning hidden meanings in particular usages, perks at their origins. Languages live and in living they change. There will be no argument from me on a line to hold.

I don't speak proper, nor often wish to, but it wasn't until I learned to that I could actually choose.

Sometimes, in academia, my own verbiage or linguistic fill-ins cause others/me to cringe. I code-switch like crazy. I get my connectors crossed. But I don't want to change, if I'm honest. I see, too often, how language is used to make others feel small when all I want is for it to be a door to a room with some seats by a fire, where words open us up, make us whole. Where they articulate the hidden corners of our hearts. So that by articulating, we can make all of the hard parts bearable.

My only wish is to pause long enough to consider words in this moment, how they affect us, how the leach and bleed of specialized language can draw us in as consumers, workers, bots, and push us away as people.

I never set out to write a dictionary; perhaps I've been successful in at least that regard. But I'm fascinated by what it means to live in this time; words like *post* and *fatigue* prick at my insides with each new iteration. After a long history, after so many advancements that were meant to ease our lives, we are after the development of the most complex societal tools in the most literate societies ever known. We are after so much, and we are tired. Exhausted, really.

B

BACKHANDED COMPLIMENT: A parent at Christmas, a sibling year-round.

BAD FAITH: Your only recourse against the bureaucratic system. So difficult to prove that the term itself seems evidence of same.[5]

[5] Modern emergencies: what starts with blood often ends in correspondence, moves from immediately necessitated response to snail mail to defensive posturing over liability. Everything was fine until it was not fine and in that *notfine* we needed to solve it. We solved it. We are adults capable of solving things. We thought.

Our provider had supplied us with a laminated card promising benefits. Empowered. Vowed protection. Suggesting safety and access. Or, for some of us, over an increasingly longer duration, we were allowed no such laminated illusions, but instead found a loophole in the emergency room, a local clinic, or somewhere we've been enough times to learn that the system's old and bendable—fungible, even—where the paperwork doesn't run so fast. Where we can outpace the bill. For now.

Or perhaps we were blessed enough to have a hospital VIP platinum frequent-fever-flier status, but our procedure was not covered by our policy because we were out of network, have failed to use a network provider. We are so ungrateful. Look at this network they provided us, but a referral or preauthorization was required, and we had typographical errors and policy limitations and a general lack of timeliness. Or we had a preexisting condition, because we find ourselves in the rare situation of having preexisted. Or maybe our procedure was considered experimental, cosmetic, investigational, or not medically necessary. Did we really have to arrive by helicopter? Just who do we think we are when we're unconscious?

Appeal? Sure we can. Please do. They've got a whole department for the 0.05 percent of all claims that get overturned. We give them our time. Come home after work and get our papers straight before we call and wait on hold for hours. Don't get the dinner ready and don't call the kids downstairs and do stress-fight with our significant other should we have one, and no, we can't speak to a manager who's currently always on break, and yes, they are recording because you never know when we might lose our cool and say something inflammatory or incriminating.

BALKANIZATION: A real conflict with real people reduced to a shorthand for fragmentation, because a phrase can travel further, wider, and longer than the events that inspired it.[6]

BANDWIDTH: The total transmission capacity of a finite system; also, *emotional bandwidth*, a phrase that suggests the human nervous system is equally finite. Normally referred to in context that one has exceeded it. Also, reducing personhood to a computing function.[7]

---

6 And we never wanted kids. We'd said that. Often. Then she began to change her mind. Not all of a sudden, I just sort of watched it happen over a period of years. It was a growth in her understanding of herself that was hard not to envy. By contrast, my own position was so entrenched that it threatened to pause me in place forever. My own story was my example of *why* I would never have a child, and a handy reason to throw about when these conversations began. I knew enough to know, too, that I could never have a child *for* someone else, that this was a recipe for disaster. Sarah did as well. So we proceeded as-if, knowing that soon this was going to be a point we would not get past.

7 There is simply not enough room, in me, for you.

BASIC: Is there anything more basic than thinking you're not?

BASTARD: A name so old and well-worn that it scarcely belongs here . . . [8]

BINARY: There are two types of people in the world. Those prone to reductive binaries . . . [9]

BLACKBALL: Nothing for you here. Keep on moving.

---

8 but so central to your narrator as to misrepresent without it.

9 and ______________________.

BLACK SITE: A geographical exception whereby a country might engage in acts they feel are counter to their principles. The governmental equivalent of "What happens in Vegas . . ." SEE ALSO: *EXTRAORDINARY RENDITION IS THE NEW ORDINARY RENDITION*. Note: seafaring vessels in international waters might not be considered black sites due to loopholes in maritime law. Plan accordingly.

BLINDSPOT: That we all have them.

BRAND: Historically, a mark placed on animals to signify ownership; later, a distinction made toward corporate alignment; now, a reinvention of the self solely as a business entity whereby living is measured in relation to alignment with corporate stratagems. Tomorrow, a mark placed on humans to signify ownership.[10]

---

10 When we'd met, I was in sales and Sarah was an elementary school teacher; she loved the kids but struggled with the politics. I knew so little of teaching that at first I thought she was joking when she said so. But between the school board, the teachers' union, the PTAs, and the old guard of teachers who saw it more as a check than a calling, she found she had little time to help kids learn. She moved into educational publishing as a solution. Then the layoffs began.

By my mid-twenties, I had a sales job that paid me so much I knew I could never quit; you might be surprised how little that was. But it was more than anyone in my family had ever made and that felt like a lot. Brand management, essentially. Cardboard. Plastics. Styrofoam. Shipping air, we called it. I was miserable, but I also knew that I'd never leave. I'd have to be fired or laid off. When they eventually did let me go, I was ecstatic.

In the months before that, I'd tried to write a memoir as part of my earnest exploration about my not wanting kids. To explore what had happened. I got up every day at 4 a.m. for a month to write before work, and after, had a full draft I was proud of. I'd stuck with it. Soon, however, one thing was clear to me above everything else: it was not at all good. Truly. So I decided to use the money work had sent me packing with and my newfound freedom to go back to school to learn how to write it right. I started taking classes at our local community college, cobbled together a plan.

Sarah had a friend who was teaching in Kuwait and bragged often about the exchange rate, like friends sometimes do. And in her own brief jobless window, Sarah threw out a line, considered giving teaching one last shot. Perhaps, she thought, in an international setting, the pressures might be different. Not long after, we loaded most everything we owned in one of those oversized boxes that arrives at your house one day and then goes away somewhere until you need it again. It's still out there today, somewhere, an entire house worth of stuff, waiting for when we start real life again.

BRAND AMBASSADOR: A modern update to the official envoy acting on behalf of a head of state, to include instead any average person, sans qualifications, on behalf of, say, potato chips.[11]

---

[11] The Towers sit within a walled compound in Mahboulla, an Indian enclave in the southern suburbs of Kuwait City. When we arrived in 2012, the neighborhood was a half-built town under constant construction. Positioned equidistant from the highway and the Gulf, it had all the chaos of a boomtown. People drove without care for lots or signs; many entered the highway through a car-sized hole in a fence rather than drive around a curve to the onramp. There were no sidewalks.

Groups of men would walk to the mosque to play cricket or uncharacteristically organized games of tug-of-war, which from my fourth-floor apartment window, I first mistook as schoolyard fights. A circle of cheers with some unseen commotion at the center. Later, I'd notice that they trained by tying a rope to a lamppost and pulling in a team of eight while someone yelled motivation at them. I wanted in, badly, but when we tried once we were rebuffed.

When it rained a small flood would wash the trash down the center of what was used as a road, presumably pouring into the next neighborhood. It was a neighborhood on the brink of becoming something—a trend not lost on me—but what was still to be determined. Locals said that the town name translated to *the mad woman,* though nobody could explain exactly which type of *mad* she was. The nuance lost.

The compound walls were twelve feet high topped with barbed wire and broken bottles. A security gate blocked the lone entrance and exit, which was manned twenty-four hours a day. A row of seven shacks lined the inside of the north compound wall, housing a team of seven Indian men, known collectively as the *haris,* who were responsible for the upkeep and maintenance of the building.

Within the walls, a further subdividing wall split the full-square-block property in half. On the other side of which, beyond a locked and gated area, was a large elaborate house, a mansion by U.S. standards, and a vibrant green grass lawn that the owner of the American school used once every few months for parties.

In our first days there, the jetlag was relentless, punishment for each invisible vertical line crossed. There was often little more than a vague notion of an endless predawn when I'd wake for the umpteenth time on any odd night. I'd look for signs out the windows that could confirm when it was: the morning water truck outside the compound's back gate, pumping to the roof; dawn's call to prayer playing through an old worn-out speaker; traffic filling the highway outside my window. But signs of time had stopped having meaning, especially in isolation from everyone we knew. I had neither job nor prospects when I arrived. This was, indeed, starting over. I was told I could be a teacher, but, without any qualifications, it would have to be *arranged*. But oh, how free we felt just then. Free of commitments, free to pursue passions.

BRAND AWARENESS: A friend has taken to saying that things are very *on brand* for them, but lacks significant brand awareness in doing so, unless the point of the brand is to repel people. Like DEET. For me, creates no sense of—

BRAND LOYALTY: That a brand deserves anything like loyalty is perhaps the best marketing scheme ever, though perhaps it is disloyal to say so.

BREAKING NEWS: Yes, a little more each time you say it; a study in diminishing returns.

BUFFERING: A fru . . . s . . . t . . . rat . . . ing . . . ly . . . sl . . . ow . . . lo . . . . ad time.

BURDEN-SHARING: A writers' workshop. A needy holiday card. Someone too long at a bar. Also, which sibling gets the parental unit—and for how long—once they are deemed redundant.[12]

BUREAUCRACY: Possibly the defining characteristic of late-stage Capitalism, though I can't say for sure; that's not my department.

---

12 We have friends, early adopters of the in-home AI technology, who work for the federal government. At an oversized house outside of DC, we spend a holiday with them instructing Alexa to wow us with audible recounts of the ingredients in an old-fashioned, how long the conflict in Syria has been going on, and how many stars the local Mexican restaurant has. After Alexa chimes in with what time the storm is coming in, Sarah looks at me as if to say: See! *Con—Ven—Ience!* But all I can do is wonder how it is possible that they are using Alexa in their house? Maybe they don't work where I thought they work after all. This is what being friends with them is like. Always. But then I think: Oh, wait, maybe their job requested that they use Alexa in their house, as like, a job requirement; a suggestion that is not a suggestion. I don't know where I fall on this. I'm not crazy. I know there is a line here. But how far? How far? I don't want to be paranoid, or worse, not paranoid enough.

BURNOUT: The body as a fuse that can be overloaded. Do you feel alienated by words, set aside or apart, less than whole? Does the way we use language, jargon, make you feel like a product, or a computer, or only important as a customer? This moment. Constantly dehumanized on a low-grade level by language.[13]

BUSINESS PARK: All business—no park.

BYSTANDER EFFECT: Are you really just going to stand there and watch this unfold?[14]

---

13 I get things done during the day:

NOT AT ALL SLIGHTLY SOMEWHAT A LOT

14 I'd protest protesting if it didn't present such a conundrum to do so. I'd write signs espousing the sign's ineffectiveness, indicting both the gloss of various substrates and the sheen of the language employed. I'd place the signs only where they obfuscated meaning. Juxtaposition. Irony. I'd arrange meetings that never met, always rescheduling—in solidarity—at the last minute. I would bemoan the bureaucratic process, in triplicate, sending each copy to the Department of Those Least Likely to Read It. If I believed that protesting did anything, I would write my congressman, impugning the fallibility of letters and those who write them. Until, that is, my own water was poisoned, and I lost the privileged position of any other option.

C

~~cancel culture:~~ Come for the accountability; stay for the mob mentality. Also, an airport at Christmas.

CAN'T STOP, WON'T STOP (PHRASE): Because there is nothing sexy or fun about *could stop, did stop*, no sense of narrative possibility.

CAPTCHA: Prove you're not a robot by noting what's wrong with this entry.

CAPITAL PUNISHMENT: Nothing *capital* about it, said the prisoner.

CARBON FOOTPRINT: Most dream of having an effect on the world; Americans do it at four times the global average.

CAREMONGERING: YOU WILL TAKE THIS HELP!

CASE SENSITIVE: Anyone who's ever caught a case.

CATCH-22: In a perfect world, the top of the eighth inning.

CATFISHING: To pretend to be someone else online.[15] Not noodling, per se, though both versions involve ripping something out of its relative safety into the cold light of a harsh world.

SEE ALSO: *KITTENFISHING*

CHAIN, DAISY: Because we all are connected.

CHAIN DISTRIBUTION SCHEME: Because not all connections are perceived in earnest. The chain letter is rebirthed as the pyramid scheme is again rebirthed as multi-level marketing. Not sales, but recruitment.[16]

[15] My fear when I find a website about my father on which I find a post that states, "This man is my father and wants nothing to do with me. Contact me if you have any information." It takes two beats to move from earnestly wanting to help to defensive questioning. But what if it's him, I think, looking for us?

[16] Repost this post if you believe reposting posts proves nothing.

CHAPTER 11: There are six chapters of bankruptcy in the U.S. financial code; 11 gets all the glory. Nevertheless, the one type of debt we will never forgive, because it would not align with our values as a country—it's just not who we are—is . . . student debt. What would it say to the kids if we did? That we support their lifestyle? Please. Further proof that financial institutions, vehicles, and laws are great at—

CHERRY-PICKING: A process for harvesting fruits and mistruths for consumption, the latter of which feeds through a selection filter to support preferred positions.[17]

CHICK CULLING: A process in industrialized egg production where redundant baby male chickens are fed through a macerator. Another cherry-picking entirely.[18]

CHYRON: The scrolling digital banner can only deal in reduction, divided attentions. That's the point.

CIRCUMLOCUTION: A terrible thing to say about a dictionary. Point taken.

---

17 The request made to amateur researchers of the original *Oxford English Dictionary* by James Murray in *An Appeal to the English-Speaking and English-Reading Public* was this: "Make a quotation for every word that strikes you as rare, obsolete, old-fashioned, new, peculiar, or used in a peculiar way. Take special note of passages which show or imply that a word is either new and tentative, or needing explanation as obsolete or archaic, and which thus help to fix the date of its introduction or disuse." Ours here might look more like this: What words can you not avoid? Which words de-center personhood in the name of business, military, or systems? Where creeps the jargon? What words hold some manipulation at the core of their modern usage? Close your eyes, dear researchers, and feel for the words that make you twitch or nearly collapse from irony when you hear them. Let's collect and construct of them a great mirror.

18 Culling animal populations is not remarkable in itself, but birthing them to kill them, as a form of regular process, defies the underlying purpose of a cull. Culling, then, in this case, is a lie we sell ourselves in order to have readily accessible eggs and cutlets, guilt-free. *Birth-to-butcher* doesn't quite appetize the same way, say, *farm-to-market* does.

CITIZENS UNITED: If in the United States a corporation is a person, then January 21, 2010, is the corporation's date of birth. As of this writing, this child is ten years old and acting like it.

CLEAN COAL: Oxymorons get a bad rap. Live recordings. Same difference. Jumbo shrimp. Together alone. A clean version of that which annually kills 50,000 workers in the United States alone. Clean like soap. Clean like morally right or neutral. Clean as in not dirty, like coal dust, for example.

CLICKBAIT: www.enticingimagesorwordspositionedtogarnerre-sponse.xin.[19]

CLIMATE CHANGE: A lobster slowly boiling on a stove, while another, much bigger lobster is stirring the pot, gently whispering, *But it's cyclical . . .*

CLOUD, THE: I'm fairly positive that belief in god is different than belief in *the cloud*, I just can't figure out how.

CODE-SWITCH: As needed, y'all.

COGNITIVE LIFT: That the weight of the mental task is relative to the gravity of the mind.

---

[19] FREE Click here to be FREE: Your Tax Refund Is Waiting: Don't delay file today, your non-account is waiting, non-accountants are standing by. Gotta upload to download, gotta spend money to make money work for you. Give us your W-2, ready your W-4s, let us WD-40 your whole tax situation. Your liability, plus our *lie*-ability, equals plausible deee-nyyy-ability. It all adds up, the numbers don't get caught lying down in an exploitable loophole of presidential proportions. Prices ultimately determined at print and likely to vary by region, refunds subject to change the subject, guaranteed examples not necessarily representa-tive of your final outcome. All testimonials are real though the photo of the blonde is illustrative only.

COMFORT ZONE: The couch, your mom's house, and the middle of a meal. SEE ALSO: *WHEELHOUSE*.[20]

---

[20] After a month in Kuwait, I got a lead on a job working as a staff writer for a bilingual magazine with an iconic name that I recognized from the states. A satellite office perhaps, I thought. Eventually I'd discover that there was no connection to the American brand and that even this subterfuge of brand recognition was a very local thing you just get used to.

The owner and I met at a café on the Gulf Road, rather than at the magazine's headquarters, and sat outdoors. The scene looked like you'd recognize from American movies when spies meet. The boss looked aging but youthful, more like an actor than anything else. He was affable—charming, even—and refused to take off his sunglasses. He sat deeply relaxed in an armed chair of metal and plastic with his knees spread as wide as his frame would allow. Peak casual. In a year, there would be a term for this approach to male physical space, but it didn't exist yet. He seemed more interested in the vibe we were having than anything approaching previous experience. Perfect, I thought.

COMPARTMENTALIZATION: A warm womb of non-consideration; a box—or many—in which to place all that which won't help one in daily life. Effective and necessary. Please don't open this box.[21]

[21] Abuelitas are the worst. Tiny, embarrassed-for-you bodies of belonging who clearly see your inchoate chameleon, liquor you at the corner store between the sunflower seeds and the saladitos, harangue you with their aggressive hands and mother's-mother gaze, interrogating your eye color, if-this-why-that-ing the skin juxtaposition, sensing deep your unrooted mezcla already.

Pobrecito, they say, confirming you don't understand, pinching your arm and slapping your cheek in loving frustration through the crowded aisles and over-burdened shelves of the local while you mutter, *No hablo*, or worse, poquito what you should have poco'd, though it takes years to know the little difference of little, while they laugh their knowing laughs at your learned ignorance.

Dios mio, their old gray hair rages at your lost culture, begrudges you because you are their own children's willful decision to forget, to tuck heritage tightly in husks and holiday packaging, some masa nacimiento nativity candles smoothing over the bumps of difference with that slickened glide of assimilation and god forbid they ask you your name that waves the white flag of erasure, easing your entrance in some rooms prior to arrival but in others, a billboard for all the things they should never have allowed in generation-slow, glacial acquiescence.

Payaso, the abuela chorus sings as it always does while you giggle and humble-weasel out of her tight grip in your practiced performance of don't-care-you've-been-called-that-so-much and awkward backwards shuffle out the mercado and when your best friend, whose parents wouldn't let you in the house last week for being too brown, asks you, *What's that lady going on about?* or *Do you know her?* you just say, *Dunno* and hold it somewhere small and deep.

COMPASSION FATIGUE: I am too tired, you see, to care about you. I have spent all of my compassion. What does it mean to simply live in a time where this exists as a codified idea, a shorthand, when we can so clearly articulate our inability to care for each other?[22]

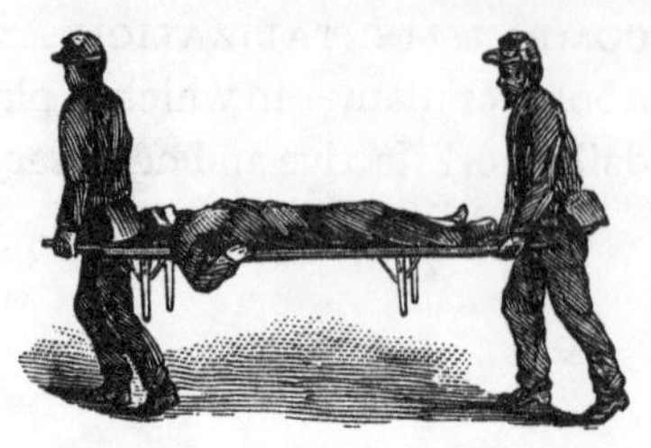

COMPLIMENTARY: aka rolled into the price.

COMPLIMENT SANDWICH: An information-delivery trick—praise, critique, then praise again—so that the person doesn't get too upset about the meat of it.[23]

CONVENIENCE CHARGE: Only facetious if you believe the convenience was ever meant to be yours.

COORDINATED INAUTHENTIC BEHAVIOR: Awkward self in mirror reflecting off a second mirror, at a party.

CORONAVIRUS: A family of viruses including the common cold, that some scientists date back at least 10,000 years, though newer molecular clock analysis suggests millions.[24]

---

22 How many ways can we say that we are incapable of feeling for each other?

23 In nearly all cases, sandwiches are named after that which is found in between the bread and not after the bread itself. (Don't worry—I see you Panini!) One assumes that an "Insult Sandwich" was at some point determined to be less digestible.

24 Barely even noteworthy unless novel.

COST AVOIDANCE: Spending less is nearly identical to earning more, if you take out the fun, life-experience, *living* bit of it all, anyway.[25]

COST PROHIBITIVE: In capitalism, the metric by which doing is measured.

COUNTERNARRATIVE: The only force in the world as strong as narrative, but only because it's also narrative.

CRISIS ACTORS: And what if you couldn't believe even what you saw with your own eyes? Then how great would your mistrust be?

CROWDFUNDING: The new American healthcare plan.

CRYPTOCURRENCY: I mean, if you can't trust a bank, who can you trust?

---

25 I purchased a car from an American who was leaving town in a hurry. It was an imitation jeep, the kind that looked like it could off-road but struggled to handle mall parking lots. What had been a deal started to look like something else. I learned to drive in Los Angeles, and it prepared me well for the rather reckless roads of Kuwait. The Middle East had, at the time, one of the highest traffic-death rates in the world, and Kuwait was high for the region.

We get a membership at the spa at the local Hilton because this is what expats do. It's luxurious. It's not the type of thing we'd splurge on at home, but because Sarah's job comes with an apartment, we have more free cash than we otherwise would. This is one of the main perks of international teaching, best I can tell. It was looking like I'd be offered a job teaching at the school. One I was unqualified for and didn't want, but that they often gave to teachers' spouses.

Once, in these early days, en route to the Hilton, I see a man, traditionally dressed in local attire, walking through the desert. It's somewhere near 120 degrees out. As I approach, he peers inside at me, sticks his thumb out. It's hot. I don't envy his walking.

I stop and let him in, flinging open the door with my right hand as I lean over. Once in he says a few words in Arabic. We drive less than 100 yards before the awkwardness begins. He says something I can't respond to. I advise him that I don't speak the language. He looks at me, confused. Perplexed. Didn't realize I wasn't local, or worse, didn't realize I was American. He starts waving his hands downward, which seems a signal for me to stop the car. I do. He gets out. He'd rather walk. We weren't even to the road yet.

CUSTODY: A protective care, but often neither.[26]

---

[26] The visitors arrive disheveled. The visitors remind each other of the rules in the parking lot. A brother tells a brother *no duh* because as visitors, they're on edge no matter how many times they've come. The sister fixes the front of a dress she'd normally not wear. Other visitors will be sent home. Several are newbies who think they're guests. Ironwood Maximum Security Hilton, presumably. One visitor brought a newborn and doesn't like how the guards check the diaper bag. When they search her in another room, the others look "better her than me." Some will be sent away because their inmate is not taking guests today. The younger brother visitor considers how that makes the prisoners sound like royalty, and how both are positions of status often conferred at birth.

The clocks wind or unwind depending on where you stand. The guards screen until a clipboard convinces them they've done their job. The guards are concerned that the term *guard* is too passive. *Corrections officer*, then, is a blanket. The corrections officer will not open one door until the previous door is closed. For these moments, which happen several times per visit, visitors are prisoners of process.

The prisoner will stand on the line. The prisoner will wait for the door. The prisoner won't touch the visitor. The prisoner must show his hands in the photo or the photo can't be taken. The photographer is a prisoner with special privileges. The prisoner cannot have a copy for himself, or, depending which prison we're at now, can be given the photo at a later date. The visitor struggles to keep track. The officers keep track of struggles. The visitor must not be late but cannot be early because they keep the doors locked around here. The visitors must possess no paraphernalia, which bans some colors and all logos; little brother kisses goodbye Raiders jerseys, god's love, and appeals to logic.

The guests are kids here to see their father. The father is a stepfather, but it didn't seem to matter till now. The inmate asks about your mother because inmate is a temporary roommate situation. The mother doesn't know you are still coming for visits. The visitors will carry no items with them except change for the vending machine. That is too much change for the vending machine. The visitor will not have an attitude about it. The prisoner will watch his mouth. The prisoner will watch his step. Watch this.

The visitors will not speak to each other. The families will not embrace. If the corrections officer has to tell you again the prisoner will lose privileges. The inmates who are grown men will stop looking at your sister. The corrections officers who are also grown men will please

stop looking at your sister. The inmates have five minutes. The convicts have all day. The latter a pejorative hurled at someone who's not going anywhere. The inmate is twitchy. The inmate is not who you remember he is within these walls. The inmate can't control you from here and maybe you can make a relationship out of that. The inmate's sure of it. The guest has his doubts. The convict's lawyer has a plan of appeal. The testimony of a surprise witness will complicate the plan. The inmate is the only guilty man he knows. The prison is far.

The visitors are tired. The prison is at the border on purpose. The visitors had to leave before dawn to be there on time but not early. The ex-visitors still have a long drive home. The kids are pulled over out front where the local police sit in wait for anyone visiting the convicts. The cop, who is a grown man, eyes the little sister in a way that nearly gets the older brother pulled out of the car. The brother should watch his mouth. Watch this: the system's an ocean. A case is a wave that crashes on the prison floor, the undertow but overture. We wade in its waters, awaiting recede. Sporadic dispatches from a sailor at sea come collect; if you'd like to accept, press 3.

DARK MATTER: The jokes we tell to keep from crying.

DAYCARE: If they cared about your day at all, this would cost less. **SEE ALSO:** ***LATCHKEY KIDS***.[27]

[27] Sarah instructs me that if there is anything I want, I'm now supposed to tell Alexa, who will pass the information on as she sees fit. It's no punishment. She plans on doing the same. Mainly she means fetching something from the store, or reminders, but it sounds more ominous to me. I ask her to tell me things the old-fashioned way, not because I'm trying to be difficult, we just don't have the same connection that they do; she doesn't push to my phone. We proceed accordingly, however, and begin randomly shouting out low-level needs whenever they occur to us.

I will be reading, say, and hear someone request the weather report, despite an increasing track record proving Alexa's inability to grasp the quickness of change in our local weather systems. My son shouts out a Pokémon question. Alexa, too, chimes in unprovoked with an occasional announcement that she has determined we need to hear. The ridiculousness of this weighs on me, and because it's how I have learned to deal, I begin to make jokes with it. *Alexa, add kisses for my wife to the grocery list.* I swear, the first time this happens she genuinely seems to enjoy it.

DAYLIGHT SAVINGS: An agreement by which millions of people simultaneously pretend the literal time is one hour sooner than it otherwise is for a portion of each year. Also, saves no daylight.

DEBTOR'S EXAM: A public shaming over an inability to pay, for example, medical bills every few months.

DELIVERABLE: Something tangible due by a definitive date: spreadsheets, food, or babies.[28]

---

[28] Getting things started on my own is important to me:

NOT AT ALL SLIGHTLY SOMEWHAT A LOT

DEMONIZE: A government can do whatever it wants if it can convince you to hate someone. Aren't we sick of being convinced, even just a little?[29]

---

[29] We were constantly aware of the rhetoric in the news, a rising feeling of regional tensions. While I couldn't read the daily paper in Arabic, I could see enough of the news in English, primarily the BBC and a few things from the States, to know that things were escalating in a general and vague way. Arab Spring was making governments nervous. It was hard not to feel the tension in the streets. You would go to the grocery store, say, and be terribly embarrassed by what a politician had said about all Muslims that day. Or perhaps you know that, just across the border into Iraq, your country has just bombed the suspected whereabouts of a *known* terrorist. You become increasingly aware of the flight path of hypothetical bombs between bickering countries. You feel the guilt of things you never said. You recognize your position as a stand-in for all of your kind. If you're not careful, you can actually start to think that people are different from each other. Us and them. Them and us. You alone.

The auto souk was ten minutes south of Mahboulla, a few long blocks of mechanics shops of all sorts. Some are brick and glass buildings, some little more than shacks with a hole in the ground for a guy to work underneath a car. Half bazaar and half auto depot, it smelled of grease and oil, screamed of engine revs and clamoring. I brought my car down while it could still putter enough to make it.

I crawled the car down the street amid bumper-to-bumper traffic, found an empty auto bay, and began to approach. As my eyes adjusted from the sun to the shade within, a guy was revealed inside, near the back, fussing about the shelves. We chatted with hand gestures and waves for a minute or two, as I tried to get him to the car. He followed me out, and I explained what I thought was wrong with it. An elaborate game of charades that even garnered the smirks of a passerby or two. Overheating was the main thing: I produced a hiss, and raised my hands like smoke from the radiator. The man nodded. He seemed old and tired. Was he happy for the business or tired of the hassle? I couldn't be sure. A knock in the engine that sometimes popped to something louder, I tried to express, imitating the sound on the hood. A troublesome oil leak. I balled my hands into fists and then extended the fingers out simultaneously while making a dropping motion, leaning down as if from under the car. Rain fingers, I thought.

After we'd agreed upon the work, he wrote a number on a receipt pulled from the pocket of his *thawb*, a number in dinars, so I had to quickly do the math in relation to the dollar. We agreed, though I was pretty sure my math was wrong. I also was keenly aware that the expectation was that I'd haggle, and by not doing so, I'd made a mark of myself. Still, I didn't have the stomach for it.

I inquired when I should come back, walking my fingers across my hands, first away, then back again. It took a few times to get this. He held up three fingers, and then, placing his hand in what could almost seem like a karate chop were it in motion, waved it in a circular fashion three times and said *Inshallah.* I had not been in the country long enough to recognize the phrase yet. He looked at me blankly and repeated the words. Three fingers, karate wave, Inshallah. Inshallah.

Someone in the street had to translate it. The answer, I would learn, was the international answer of car mechanics everywhere. *He says your car will be ready in three days—god willing.* A lovely little confirmation, I thought, that we're all the same everywhere.

DE-NAMING: A corrective, often excoriated by sufferers of "glory day syndrome" or any of its co-morbidities. If you or someone you know needs help, please call 1-719-266-2837. Operators are standing by.[30]

[30] That Chaucer is the founder of modern English is a theory that divides scholars into different camps. It seems none disagree that his era was at least a pivotal time for English and his work was consequential. One of the reasons cited is the number of words from the French that he puts into common usage in English for the first time in his writings: 1,180, though later some scholars will wish to take 177 of these back. Others think his work just reflects the time he was writing. He was using an English that was already antiquated, and because of that, his usage could be seen as reminiscent of another, better time. Something was being lost. He was saving it. Make English Great Again. We love that one. Then others followed suit, claiming that he was now the barometer to measure to or risk losing the language; others jumped onto his usage for their own political purposes. Language use has always been political.

DENSIFICATION: When seats are packed so closely together on a plane that it is inevitable that people will have conflict.[31]

DESENSITIZE: How the corporation abstracts people in the name of serving them.[32]

---

31 January 12, 2020, an average day: on an American Airlines flight, a middle-aged man, balding, bearded, and bespectacled, begrudgingly sits in the least preferred seat of an airplane—the last row, aisle seat, 21D. A woman from Virginia sits down in 20D immediately in front of him. There are details that look like humanity: at some point in the flight, she reclines her seat. At some point, wanting to eat, he requests that she raise it, and she obliges. At some point, he finishes eating, and she, likely having felt she had fulfilled her communal obligations toward mutual comfort, of give and take, lowers her seat again. His row, of course, doesn't recline at all, and it is quite possible that he, trapped and disgruntled, might feel the proximity is a violation of his limited personal space. 21D is likely aware, however, that 20D has had no part in either designing this plane or plotting its seating arrangement.

He begins punching the back of her seat, steadily, with no purpose other than to annoy her into raising her seat again. A flight attendant is reported to have rolled her eyes at the woman when she reported the behavior and responded by offering the man rum. The woman records the incident because she feels she has no other recourse but to capture evidence. It is so childish, it's practically presidential. Still, in the video—because I am sometimes compelled to click on such videos—it's the deadened look in his eyes that I recognize most. He is not there, tuned out. He has locked into some other mode of being that would be subhuman were it not so human. Animalistic. Rage. News reports suggest that the internet is divided on who is wrong here.

32 Customers. Users. Buyers. Sellers. Stakeholders. End users. Clients. Members. Target customers. Actors. Personas. The organizational ontology hides personhood.

DIGITAL INEQUALITY: Are you presently reaping the benefits of digital assistants, robot vacuums, and on-demand need fulfillment, or do you know only the alienation of the recorded voice whenever you attempt a phone call? Which digital life are you living?

DIMINISHING RETURNS: Whether a spoonful of ice cream or the bombing of a nation, the effect is worth less each time.[33]

DINK: Double Income No Kids. What we were until we weren't.

DISASTER CAPITALISM: Not catastrophe—opportunity. Winners and losers. SEE ALSO: *SHOCK DOCTRINE*.

DISINFORMATION: The coming election, as with the last, but worse. SEE ALSO: *MISINFORMATION*.

DISTANCING LANGUAGE: Whether by pronoun, metaphor, euphemism, deflection, or omission, whether by employing the passive or minimizing the active, or simply circumlocution until we're seasick, whether to avoid, obscure, mislead others or ourselves, we are well-trained soldiers of the accountability tightrope.

33 One day, I am sitting on the couch reading a book. My wife is looking through the fridge somewhere behind me and yells, *Alexa, add pickles to the grocery list*. She continues like this in a way that leads me to believe that she was likely trying to make a sandwich. I say my kisses line to Alexa, or some variation, which is fine, apparently, though the charm is wearing off. Did she groan? My son, too, has caught on. Adds snuggles. Adds take a bath with our dog. Adds hot dogs. I can follow his logic.

DNA TEST: Over-the-counter DNA kits become the norm. And though there is a legacy of books that warn of the government having this information, many of us give it freely—no, *pay* for the opportunity—to know something more about ourselves. There is something we don't know about ourselves that we think an over-the-counter kit can tell us. And I take one also, because I too want to know. Tell me. In record time, the government begins using it to convict people.[34]

DONOR FATIGUE: Not feeling exhausted after giving your sample for the DNA test, but a threshold, nevertheless, where one is too tired to give any more.

DOOMSCROLLING: In doomed times we just call this scrolling.

DO WHAT YOU GOTTA DO ***(PHRASE)*****:** Justification in progress.

---

34 Meanwhile, the number of untested rape kits alone is high enough to make you think the technology doesn't exist in any feasible way. At the time of this writing there are 2,300 untested kits in Texas, where I'm writing. And my natural reaction is, wow, that's not as many as I would have thought. Is that jaded? Is that callous? Is this what progress looks like and I've just not noticed? I check California and it's 13,000. I check New York City and apparently, they've stopped giving the statistic. That sounds more like what I would expect. Later, a professor who also works on legal cases in the state of Texas tells me that the state is lying about the number anyway. It's way more than this, she says.

I take a DNA kit, because I too want to feel what a whole, inarguable truth might feel like. The comfort of a fact. DNA facts turn out not to be the comfort I thought they would be. I'm still waiting to be comforted.

Later, a detective contacts one of my sisters to inquire what she knows about our father. In the midst of a high-risk pregnancy, she feels too weak to talk. She's worried about the stress of it, so she asks me to call him back instead. Of course, I say. When I do call—they refuse to speak to me about it. There's no record of me; no proof that I'm his son. I suggest that they call any of my many siblings, newfound or old, for verification. It doesn't matter, the detective won't speak to me.

DOXING: One's digital life leveraged against one's physical one, for either good or evil, determined at the whims of the wielder.

DO YOURSELF A FAVOR *(PHRASE)*: Surest way to guarantee I won't be taking your advice.[35]

DROSTE EFFECT: In art, an image going on forever forever forever forever.

DRUG TESTING: What a judge, employer, or potential employer might require, but not only.[36]

DRUG TRAFFICKING: I mean, that's one way to make traffic tolerable.

---

35 Unsolicited advice is peak this moment: the preemptive *You're welcome,* when no thanks was given; or *Not sure who needs to hear this, but*—when everyone seemed to be getting on fine without it. In person, it feels like the casual recommendation of a friend. There is a down-home wisdom about it. Online, it seems like someone believes they're blessing you. It's the eyes I really fear for. How will we ever account for all of the eyeballs that roll out of people's heads in response?

36 At eighteen, one of my roommates was a nurse in training at a local doctor's office. She told me I could get a couple hundred dollars for taking some unknown drugs for a few months at a time—clinical trials, they were called. All you had to do was keep a journal of how you felt while on them. This was something I pretty much did anyway, so I figured why not. Most of the drugs were allergy related, though not exclusively. Between the ramping on, the base level period, the possibility of placebo, and the ramping off, I was miserable for a year, basically with the symptoms of a cold. When I developed GI problems years later, I couldn't be sure these things weren't related.

DUMDUM: A bullet that expands on contact, purposefully, to maximize impact and potentially, a description of the user.[37]

DUNNING-KRUGER EFFECT: When you're exceptionally good at something but the world can't see it.

---

[37] On January 12, 2020, perhaps because it's average, good things happened too. Somebody helped an old lady across the street. Somebody found someone else's lost dog. A neighbor mowed the lawn of a neighbor grieving the loss of his wife. I couldn't find proof of these incidents, but they must be true, right? There are no examples when I google variations of "What good things happened on January 12?" because, Boolean logic or otherwise, I don't seem to have the right words.

I recently read that part of why we are so critical in academia—or, rather, one reason why seemingly everything defaults to critique—is that our vocabulary for being critical is so much more advanced than our vocabulary for __________. Can that be true? And what is the word, even? Is it praise? Is it support? (Quickly googles antonyms for *critique*: *complimentary* seems closest.) Is that the word?

Why don't I have the words to easily be complimentary, and why does that word feel so stiff and trite?

E

ECOLOGICAL GRIEF: A psychic response to looking out your window.

EFFICIENCY: A term to signify a desire to limit waste of energy or resources. Also, in the negative, justification for why a corporation should eliminate humans not at optimal health from the workstream. SEE ALSO: *RATIONALIZATION*.

EMAIL: A Trojan horse by which an employer can intrude into the non-work time of the proletariat. Also, a direct line between producers and consumers. Also, a wormhole one can fall into and come out of, having lost all conception of time.

EMIGRANT: If you're an emigrant when you leave your home country and an immigrant when you arrive in your new one, what are you in between?[38]

EMOJI: For all of our complex communications, sometimes the modern equivalent of a cave drawing simply feels better.

EMOTIONAL HEDGING: Expressed emotion shaped in a manner so as not to expose the speaker to unwanted vulnerability.

EMOTIONAL-SUPPORT ANIMAL: An animal companion to calm fears of existential angst. But who is comforting the animals?

---

[38] Fodder.

EMPLOYMENT INSTABILITY: You will have more jobs in your lifetime than your parents did, and your children more than you. Apparently, you do yourself a great disservice—financially, at the very least—by staying at companies even longer than 2–5 years. Don't get too comfortable.[39]

---

39 In 2012, while sitting in my apartment in Kuwait trying to decide where to spend Christmas vacation, it occurred to me that as an American, I might be running out of time to visit Russia, at least for the foreseeable future. Something in the escalation of rhetoric in the news suggested a window closing. I had always been intrigued by the culture, literary and otherwise. I wanted to go to Dostoyevsky's house. Pushkin's library. I wanted to stand in Red Square. I heard one could ice-skate in Gorky Park. And there is a certain shade of brown characterizing the Arabian Desert that after a while you can't get out of your head. You need a tree; you crave bushes and water, if only for the juxtaposition of colors. It was a day after we arrived when the Russian government announced the ban on Americans adopting babies, not that this affected us in any material way. It was in the news, perhaps, but not yet in the air.

It was Christmas Eve, late, and all the shops had begun to close. It was too frozen outside to go anywhere. Most locals we'd met—the desk clerk, the waitress, the docent at the museum for the Patriotic War of 1812— seemed to think we were crazy to vacation there in the time when even Russians left the cities for an extended winter break, when things closed down for the winter holiday. But for us it was perfect. No tourists, no frills: just us and the remaining locals eating borscht and walking the frigid city. Sarah was eager to be in a country where she thought she might be able to pass as local; her being fair skinned, this didn't happen much in the Gulf. She was shocked to find that she couldn't blend in. She simply smiled too much, like a Californian, a dead giveaway, marking us instantly as tourists. Though off-putting at first, the local commitment to not smiling was so great that it soon became charming.

I wondered if I too might have been smiling aggressively. But where she seemed a sore thumb, I, on the other hand, the ethnically ambiguous, would get spoken to in Russian, as sure as I would in Arabic back in Kuwait. On the street, the blessing of not standing out created a problem in direct proportion once social interactions began. When it was discovered I didn't speak the language, it caused more confusion, embarrassment on both sides: them for their assumption, me for my ignorance.

Sarah and I spent the holiday as couples far away from family obligations often do: celebrating ourselves, largely. Our hotel was one of the Seven Sisters, the local name for Lenin's old towers around the city, though now a Hilton. We spent an extended time in bed. We ordered room service repeatedly and I decided there was a version of beef stroganoff I could fall in love with. We watched a season of *Downton Abbey* over a ghost VPN on my computer when local TV got old, alternating between small bottles of hotel vodka and bouts of hot cocoa.

An email arrived late enough on Christmas Eve to be morning that I had gotten the staff writer position at the magazine. I was to be, it suddenly seemed to me, a *real* journalist. I jumped up and down on the bed in celebration, while Sarah tried not to spill cocoa from a small paper cup.

ENCROACHMENT: So much American anger seems to be about space, who's giving space or taking it.

ENFORCED COMPLIANCE: If it has to be forced it is not complying.

EPIGENETIC INHERITANCE: What we carry between us, through generations. Beyond just your parents, you carry your grandparents too, and theirs.[40]

ESPERANTO: If we could just speak the same language, it would be so much harder to separate us. That we need communication, understanding, and an idealistic renewal.

EUTHANASIA: Because "easy death" tells us too directly what a person might be requesting, closes the linguistic aperture to too sharp a focus. What comfort we find in the distance of the Greek, the Latinate, the vaguely floral, and the fecund potential for humor.

40 That I am not contending just with my father, but with my father's father, and his.

EXPAT: People running from something, but with greater privilege and at a more casual clip than those who must flee. (As a universal rule it won't hold; as personal anecdote, it feels right.)[41]

---

41 You have to be invited to attend the happy hour at the U.S. embassy. Westerners and locals jockey for position for this, the only place one can cut loose—except for private homes—like you otherwise might at home. The embassy rules are many and strict. You must be cleared in advance. You must be on the list. You must have your passport. You must behave yourself, not that people often do. You can drink all you want but must remember that it is illegal to be drunk once you leave embassy grounds. A taxi takes you and you can't believe how easy it is to approach, in through the front gates, slowed to a crawl through the many speed bumps, the barricades, the pylons, the first two local soldiers doing little, the next two doing less, the final two stereotypical no-nonsense Americans. You are used to being eyed suspiciously. And the zigzag, the winding, the increasingly heightened security checkpoints lead you to a portable container, which you'll think means you're in, but it's only the first check. There'll be another, and another, and then someone you know will have to personally look at you and vouch for you and say that person there is with me. Not that one—that one. And so groups are divided and subdivided and picked and claimed and denied and if you make it you don't see each other again until within earshot of a bad house band singing American rock songs with an accent so thick the words are lost. Or sometimes there's a get-together of assorted transient military men of unknown assignments. You're suddenly drinking with a wide array of military, including a general or some other high-ranking officer you think you may have just seen on TV. This is America, technically. This square mile of living quarters that resembles an average American apartment complex, not even a particularly nice one, but with severely increased security. Happy hour happens at the equivalent of the clubhouse. That's where I first met Mike (that's what we'll call him anyways), a soldier in charge of running a house for soldiers passing through slow enough that a hotel wasn't feasible, nor quick enough to justify a full move.

EXTRA MILE, *THE* (TO GO): Sales-speak for fulfilling the requirements of your job while broadcasting it as somehow exemplar. Sadly, there is no *above and beyond* or 110% either.[42]

EXTRAORDINARY RENDITION: This post has been moved to an undisclosed location.

---

42 When someone says you'd be good at sales or you'd make a great salesperson, what are they saying?

(A) You have a compelling personality that could easily manipulate people.
(B) You seem like someone consumed with self-interest.
(C) I feel a sudden need to shower and/or watch my purse or wallet.

What I'm getting at here is that it is not a compliment. The salesman is a pariah, a con artist. The salesman talks on his phone too loudly, prompted by self-importance. The salesman travels to and fro, scorched-earthing in the name of his own self-interest. He has to, really; it's the job. This is not to impugn the world of sales, but the higher I got up in it, the less clean I felt about the task, and I am telling you that I either became this person or I was this person all along. I am telling you that this was the best of a very limited set of options. I had to try, really hard, to work *up* to that thing that didn't make me at all happy. And that when others told me it was the best chance for someone like me, which seemed to only ever mean uneducated, without money or options—I knew they were right.

But a journalist, well, now that's another thing entirely, right? In America, the journalist is a hero, doing the legwork of the people's business. In and out of halls of power, shining lights on all the most corrupt places, the journalist is a vital cog in the machine that makes our democracy possible.

More than anything, the move was one from maximum exploitation for personal gain to one of service. Yes, I was one thing, and now I was becoming another.

F

FAKE NEWS: Initially, any news that a presidential candidate disagreed with; later, the general disposition of his administration. Lately, a catch-all term for anything said by the other side.

FALSE ADVERTISING: Saying one thing and meaning another. Like fake news. Like this book, for example.[43]

FALSE FLAG: Likely not the only contemporary political problem whose roots are rumored to trace back to pirate ships.

---

43 Around Christmas 2019, we discover that Alexa has a direct line to Santa Claus. It starts out great, if a little stilted. *Ho, ho, ho, you're on hold for Santa,* or something like it. For all our promises to our son of insider access—letters that we can pass on directly if he'd like us to, good words regarding his behavior spoken on his behalf—*this* somehow makes it more real to him. His eyes widen as he starts talking rapid-fire to Santa. For a second or two this is as perfect as you might envision it.

But he's asking too many questions, and before you know it, Santa has to go. And we need to call back because he wants to ask him something else. And when we do, the conversation is clearly recorded, is the exact same as before, and I begin to worry that the dishonesty of the whole thing is about to be revealed. By the third callback, he seems to know something is up, even if he can't quite articulate it.

FALSE FRIENDS: Cognates that are not as they seem and nearly each person my social media platforms keep suggesting to me.[44]

FEEDBACK LOOP: A literal and a metaphorical problem.

FIDUCIARY DUTY: What your tax accountant says before he does something shady.

FINE PRINT: The place in print to place that which is least likely to be fine.

FISHING FOR COMPLIMENTS: I mean, I probably don't deserve them, really. But if you say so.

---

44 In 1220, John of Garland, a medieval grammarian, coins the term *dictionary* in a book of Latin phrases. Early versions are more like encyclopedias because a dictionary evolves over time, the earliest ones often necessitated by a need to carry between languages. Some suggest the earliest is the Sumerian-Akkadian, a script found on early cuneiform tablets. The first monolingual dictionary is speculated to be the Shizhoupian dictionary from 800 BCE China, but others dismiss this book instead as a compendium. This is where I have to look up the precise definition of a compendium. I know it, but I don't *know* it. This will continue for some time: Elyot, Mulecaster, Florio, Cawdrey, Cowell, Phillips, Baley, Martin, until the English language stakes its own first claim at a unified and differentiated tongue through Samuel Johnson. Scholars seem to agree: it is not at all a first, and yet kind of a first. Such is the nature of origin stories.

FLAG-WAVING: A shallow patriotism when offered alone. Like tweeting "I love you" to a spouse: if you did you wouldn't need the world to see you do it. It means more to do it quietly. Doesn't it? Or perhaps I'm just not demonstrative about much at all. Perhaps I have antiquated notions of what it means to show care.[45]

FLASH MOB: A choreographed routine meant to seem spontaneous, whether by dancing, robbery, or otherwise.

---

45 Sarah and I begin to argue over the state of the Alexa grocery list. Whether or not it is charming to leave her messages this way, or whether it is getting out of hand. No, really, she says, this is getting out of hand.

She says she had to remove 25 things from the grocery list while in the aisle of the store yesterday. This is a playful non-fight disguised as a fight. They're generally rooted in truth, and they're certainly not to be ignored, but they're also a way that we have fun with each other.

I remind her, in jest, that I'm only responsible for half of those 25 and at 12.5 extra items, largely compliments and tiny gifts to her, mind you, I'd hardly say we're quite out of hand. She looks at me like all this hand business makes her want to slap me. Two notches above a love slap, roughly. Do I need to stress again that this is play? But the other half of the list, I mention, comes from a smaller copy of myself—that she is partially responsible for to the degree of 6.25 items—that is similarly inclined in the joke department. She says but we don't have a joke department. And why is that? I ask. Alexa, I say, start a joke department. And we are right at the line where she is done playing, and so I must be too.

She indicates that the list had something offensive on it that we both know instantly must have come from our son, stinky anything currently being a punch line to nearly all of his jokes. It is clear he wouldn't know the other word though, and this is a clerical error on Alexa's part. I try to assure her that it will be okay—he's just having fun, and the families that should worry are the ones where the husband doesn't put ridiculousness on the grocery list, and the son isn't smart enough to usurp the rules. I mention the cognitive benefits of wordplay at his age. Before I can even finish, my son runs through the room and yells, *Alexa, I am a pine cone.* Her point is made, but I'm not sure exactly how. Okay, I say. Okay.

FLOCCINAUCINIHILIPILIFICATION: A dictionary with non-literal definitions, perhaps.

FOG OF WAR: Situational unawareness at a time when one should be most aware.

FOMO: No, but really—what if something happens without me?[46]

FRACAS: A brawl in olden times or places.[47]

---

46 I am interested in having new experiences.

NOT AT ALL SLIGHTLY SOMEWHAT A LOT

47 After two weeks spent between Moscow and St. Petersburg, we had begun to prepare for our departure back to Kuwait the following morning. Living in a dry, strict country often caused a frenetic, gluttonous pace to our final vacation hours: beers, bacon, and unedited movies. We hopped in the elevator to start our search for booze to take home.

Downstairs in our hotel, the Leningradskaya, I asked the bellman to point me to the closest liquor store, holding my hand in the international shape of a cup and bringing it to my lips several times. He looked perplexed. Misread, I thought, the action might too closely resemble the sign for blowjob. *Vodka. Vodka.* I said, pointing outward to the city, pronouncing a longer and more conspicuous "O" than I'm used to in an attempt to sound local.

"You know you look like a crazy person, right?" Sarah said behind me.

"Feel free to get in here anytime, *honey*."

We tended to use terms like this mockingly, and she laughed at my tacit acknowledgment that she was right.

The bellman pointed us toward what appeared to be a deserted, impassable bridge, mimed that we should pass beneath it to the other side. It looked dark and abandoned, desolate I thought, with no signs of anything beyond but more of the same. Still, where normal people might have turned away, we pressed on out of dire need: that Sarah was an elementary school teacher likely says everything you need to know about her need to drink. For me, the *pruno* wine and pot-stilled liquor ubiquitous on our compound had given me a terrible case of rotgut, and I wasn't sure my colon could survive another batch.

We nodded our heads in agreement and poured our way down Kalenchevskaya Street, huddling against each other for warmth, exhaust fumes assaulting our already frozen noses. Sarah was bundled up so high on the neck I could only trust that she was in there, her long blond hair sticking out the back of her beanie, a waving flag of pseudo-confirmation.

Halfway through the tunnel, we began to see that we had indeed been sent in the right direction. A train station was in the near distance, a bank, some shopping ahead. We passed a government-looking building with guys, seemingly drunk, hanging outside. They didn't appear homeless, nor were they going anywhere—strange given the below-freezing temperature.

As we approached a busy intersection, we noticed a small sign portraying two clanking bottles and pointing underground, beneath which sat an ambulance, parked on the sidewalk, nearly blocking access. A crowd was forming, intently watching something unfold. I wormed my way between the bundled and huddled crowd, Sarah's hand now protectively held close to my back, as we made our way through and descended the steps.

Two paramedics walked upstairs, carrying a bloody man with a baseball-sized welt on his forehead. His mouth hung open, moist with spittle. I thought I heard the guttural sound of throat singing. We looked and tried not to simultaneously, while still descending into what could only be described as a haze, or a cloud you could feel but not see. We entered the store to find an entire aisle's worth of bottles broken on the floor, the wreckage wet, smeared, and smelling of the pungency of alcohols that shouldn't mix.

I had never previously experienced the palpable fog that exists in spaces where a large and public trauma has just happened, where a post-rage vacuum sucks out the breathable air like a collective gasp, but I could feel now that I'd stepped completely into one, the off-putting strangeness of a group ignoring what had just taken place. The store was packed: every cashier's lane five people deep, nobody acknowledging the disaster at the door, or the two guys who seemed responsible for it all, still inside, drunk and combative, wandering the aisles.

FRACKING: Both a comical attempt to not say a curse word on a 2000-era TV show and a process that strips the Earth of natural resources by gutting its insides, both to disastrous effects.

FRENCH EXIT: An often frowned-upon phrase used as justification for premature and unspoken leave-taking, where one simply picks an ethnicity or nationality—nothing ever problematic about that, of course—and a synonym for departure. SEE ALSO: *IRISH GOODBYE; DUTCH LEAVE; ENGLISH EGRESS; ROMANIAN RETIREMENT; QATARI QUIT*; and *U.S. WITHDRAWAL*.

FRENEMY: Writers at writing conferences.

FRIEND: A click of a button that can feel like more. **SEE ALSO**: *UNFRIEND*.[48]

FRIENDLY FIRE: The classification for any shooting that precedes the term *my bad*.

FUBAR: The least appealing of all bars.

---

[48] Sarah found something unexpected in Kuwait: friends she describes as the sweetest and most supportive she has ever had. Not like American girlfriends, she'll say. The friend she traveled to Kuwait to be near failed her; that relationship dissolved slowly, strained under the pressures of nothing spectacular: perceived jealousies, cattiness, new friends. Maybe something more that she wouldn't say.

Life in the teacher compound was dorm-like, an extended adolescence where many of the teachers acted like children themselves, like college freshmen, really, though they'd all finished school. The men could be childlike and immature, the women catty and cliquish. But outside of the compound walls, a random assortment of local women, largely parents of Sarah's students, and a friend who worked at the embassy became her new tightknit circle.

Sarah and I have tried to unpack the irony many times since: what seemed to restrict her, from a Western perspective—the societal restrictions placed on women, that is—actually provided her a bigger safety net and social network than she'd ever known, even more notable for simultaneously limiting my own. It is true that Kuwaiti society was closed off to foreigners in some ways. Not that they were not welcoming, but that the welcome was arm's length for many. Her role as an elementary school teacher had been a nice bypass within that arm's length. She was let in, she was embraced, whereas I, a man, or perhaps because I was a journalist, was kept distant, despite having more insider access into the upper echelons of society overall. There was a suspicion of me that could either have been due to me personally, or the fact that I was understood to be a journalist. Both make sense. She's friends with many of them still, years later, still happily follows their many life changes. When the time came, they threw her an elaborate Western-style baby shower at a chalet, replete with all of the extravagances of an affluent Kuwaiti celebration. They treated her like one of their own. All her friends. She says it was the sweetest and most thoughtful celebration she could have wished for.

G

GAMESMANSHIP: Everything is a game.

GAME THEORY: Because even if it isn't all a game, thinking of it as a game helps.[49]

GAMIFICATION: But while you're playing games about whether it's all a game or not—enticed into a new activity, a reaction, or simply clicking more buttons—someone else is making money.

---

49 A nondescript black SUV suddenly appeared across the street. Parked sideways, it screamed government issue down to the limousine-grade tint job. From my window several floors above, I could see at least four men inside. Soldiers. I'd been pacing, peering occasionally from behind the curtain of a floor-to-ceiling window that ran the expanse of my living room. Above them: a man dangled on the end of a swinging crane in repeated trips from the top to bottom of a building under construction. Others climbed up and about a rickety system of makeshift scaffolding: wood planks and posts tied with leather straps. A minaret peeked up just beyond the building. For the past twenty minutes, I'd heard the hum of a truck pumping water to my roof from just outside the compound walls. A text came in, and I took my cue to head down.

Down the steps, through the compound courtyard, past the security guard booth, and out onto the busy street. Dust kicked about with passing traffic. I timed my way through traffic to the passenger side door of the vehicle.

The driver asked if I'd be at the embassy later. Something about a party at their own compound after. *Bring people.* I thought he might mean girls. He said they were on a run back from Arafjan and he'd brought me something. As if on cue, one of the soldiers started to move his body up and over the back seat. The other soldiers didn't stop fixating on the high volume of traffic in the street; the traffic couldn't stop noticing them either. I didn't know this guy well enough to warrant gifts. An unmarked package worked its way through the car to the passenger, who handed the package out to me, face down: something wrapped in something wrapped in something else. *Keep this lo-pro.* I looked around, held it down close to my side. Disappeared it. The street bustled.

Mike lives in a four-story beachside house paid for by the U.S. government. He oversees the coming and going of a rotating cast of American servicemen who come in on smaller, specific jobs. If an IT guy, say, has to come in for a few weeks to fix computers at one of our bases, this is where he stays. If the Kuwaiti Navy needs training on some new boat, this is where the crew who trains them stays. Mike's the papa bear of the house, and he spends all his time keeping it running smoothly. If he is not running around acquiring provisions to keep the house stocked—a complicated process that requires the constant doing and receiving of favors—he is somewhere acting as security for someone high up.

I first met him at the embassy.

I liked Mike—or grew to, anyway—and I liked that he offered access to things, but here is what I thought: he was nice to me because I lived on a compound where there were many single Western women who, given the opportunity, occasionally welcomed the chance to act as so many of us would if we were at an average college party back home. Free of local laws. Free of peering eyes. Almost like home. Almost. I hurried back across the road and up into my apartment. I opened the package: bacon.

GASLIGHTING: The lights aren't flickering; perhaps the world is simply blinking around them.

GENETICALLY-ENGINEERED RODENT MODELS: Not ultra-attractive rats, but ones we test on.

GENOGRAM: The new family tree, because legacy is more than simple genealogy.

GENRE: That these distinctions matter to some and are said to not even exist by others. That there is so much genre snobbery in academia. That the best-selling genres aren't literary. That these two things are likely connected. That the adverbial form is generic.

GERRYMANDERING: People in power drawing the line however they choose and justifying it after the fact.[50]

GHOSTING: To disappear in the middl . . . SEE ALSO: *BIRDBOXING; BREADCRUMBING; ORBITING; CURVING; CUSHIONING; BENCHING; ZOMBIEING;* and *LOVEBOMBING.*

GHOST VPN: Hide who, where, and what you are because a digital trail may one day matter. In Kuwait we needed these for even very common Western sites that the ministry chose to block. One wonders how long until that will be necessary in the States.

---

50 Named after Elbridge Gerry, who dreamed a funny-shaped Boston. His name isn't actually pronounced with a soft *g* at all. So entrenched is the word in our lexicon, however, that to *Gary*-mander sounds like a totally different and inappropriate process altogether. Perhaps it's that conspicuous *man*, unable to hide in the middle of the term. Or maybe the *er* making it active as it simultaneously growls at us. Maybe it's just something in my understanding of people named Gary more broadly.

GISH GALLOP: That you can hear a bad-faith argument coming from far off but it nevertheless takes longer to disprove than to assert.

GLOBAL WARMING: Don't let the sound of approaching hooves distract from the floods and fires.

GOAT: Not a goat, in fact, great or otherwise.

GRACE: A leniency granted only by god and creditors, but often neither.[51]

---

[51] You could get caught smuggling twice before it was a problem, that was the rumor; or was it you could get caught once and the second time you were in trouble? Who knows, given the way information travels. Still, you really had to be pushing distribution amounts before that was even likely to happen. A rumor as well. Mainly, there was a hole in the system.

You show up from your flight, go to the corral to claim your bags in an oversized room with a scanner and several armed guards, nearly always exclusively men. They would watch the person go through along with their bags, sometimes watching the scanner, often watching the person. They'd say a few muttered words to each other on the side in a laughably quick conference. That was the check for contraband.

There was a restroom in the waiting area where you could go after picking up your bag but before sending the bag through the scanner. There was no scanner for people. This is where people would suit up with their alcohol. It could be done on the plane too, I suppose, but I mean, if there's space in the airport . . .

It didn't sound like smuggling. It sounded like bending a rule that shouldn't have existed to begin with. Most homes that I went into in Kuwait had alcohol; most private social gatherings did too, though certainly not the public ones. It was really a bureaucratic thing. I was told that the rule didn't exist in any form prior to the 1970s and since then has been used largely to control incoming foreigners. But to consider it as such is a privilege only afforded to those higher in the pecking order. Kuwaitis, Brits, and Americans, in that sequence, were at the top of the list.

Of course, you should honor the rules and culture of the country you are in. Of course. This is all rationalization, I know, but it's the thought process nonetheless. When we arrived back from Russia, I was not brave enough to break this rule, no matter how inconsequential it was purported to be. An essay extolling the virtues of traveling to Russia in the off season was one of my earliest pieces to get published.

GREENWASH: Giving something the appearance of being environmentally friendly without necessarily making it so. (AKA *GREEN SHEEN*)

GRIEFING: A more severe and less earnest version of trolling. SEE ALSO: *TROLLING*. ALSO: *REDEFINE EARNEST*.[52]

GRIFT: As a term, an American invention of the early twentieth century; as an idea—that people can be preyed upon and misled—as old as humanity itself; as a peak moment: now, as I write this.[53]

---

52 Alexa, I farted, my son says, several times a day for a few months. Congratulations, she responds, and a slow, singular clap rises to a roar, '80s movie style. When he tires of this, he turns instead to blaming it on her, though no flatulence has actually transpired. She alternates between claiming to not know what he is saying and offering a long scientific explanation for why this is not possible. Sometimes, instead, she suggests he recalibrate his voice so she can better understand him.

53 The word *grift* first appears in the 1914 dictionary *Vocabulary of Criminal Slang*. A recent *New York Times* article suggests that there is something distinctly American about grifters, while also noting that they traditionally have existed in the margins of societies. This article distinguishes between, for example, "conniving politicians" and "grifters," because the former is part of the system, whereas the latter is outside of it. But what if that weren't so? What if a grifter somehow became the center?

GUILT: The feeling that you may be responsible is not always tied to knowing, factually, that you are not.[54]

GULF WAR SYNDROME: What must American Syndrome look like to, say, an Iraqi?

---

54 The small office of the magazine was a painfully hip place, music on too loud, foosball in the corner. Red Bull girls stopped by to stock a Red Bull–branded mini fridge with a regularity meant to imply importance. My desk was one over from the one stuck beneath a stairwell that went nowhere, led to a ceiling tile. My coworkers and I were a decidedly multinational bunch: one Kuwaiti, one Egyptian, one Lebanese, two Indians, one man whose national origin escapes me, one Kiwi, and me, the American. There was a sense about the place that, even though the work we were doing was largely forgettable—a lifestyle magazine—there was an importance to us doing it together. As the Western voice, I was brought in to push on conservative society, but only slightly. My first piece was on "Yo mama" jokes for Arab Mother's Day, a subject that all seemed to think could be funny, although several thought it went too far. I asked them to let me try, and they did. No censors showed up.

Because the pressures of the Arab Spring were beginning to flame all around us, the government increased its pressures on the media, the censors watched, and we were always aware of it. The government imposed a mandatory ten-year prison sentence and a 100,000 dinar fine for even tweeting anything negative about the emir. At an exchange rate of 3.5 to 1, this fine was more than the cost of many homes in the United States, where I was hoping to eventually return. The effect was chilling, but still we pushed.

Whenever a terrorist attack happened anywhere in the world, there was a deafening silence in the room. We'd all rush to our computers to start researching the details, calling them out audibly when we learned anything new. Then, inevitably, came an answer to a question that nobody ever asked. It caught me by surprise when I first heard it articulated: *Thank god—It wasn't one of us.*

By us, they meant Muslim. Make no mistake, there is no way any of them would be mistaken for anything approaching fundamentalist, perhaps not even conservative. The office was remarkably liberal, a few outliers aside, certainly less religiously zealous than many companies I'd worked for in the States. But the heaviness of the *us* stayed with me. They felt in some way implicated in crimes done on behalf of their religion. Not because they are, of course not. Of course not. But because they know—intrinsically— the binary implied. Each of us, keenly aware of the things we don't want done being done on our behalf.

HALF-BREED: One who is half. No more. What they used to call that unknowable thing they see about you. Is society changing, or are they just quiet about it now? The amalgam. The hybrid, half-caste, hodgepodge, bifurcated mishmash miscegenation. Mestizo mixed breed, Green bean, mixed blood. Am I a slash or am I a hyphen; am I half or a whole person? Are we half or are we both? Is it duality then? Maybe two things. Twice as connected to culture. Twice as aware of our stance. If pushed, I will defensively assert that we're both, but most days, inside, I feel half.

HARDWIRED (AKA PROGRAMMED): That a person is a fixed digital entity whose functions can't be undone.[55]

---

[55] I am interested in learning new things

NOT AT ALL	SLIGHTLY	SOMEWHAT	A LOT

HARRISON, CHASE: A toddler, born Dmitry Yakovlev but also known as Dima, who died in 2008 after being left in the car seat of his newly adoptive parents' car for nine hours, just three months after arriving in America. Namesake of the Dima Yakovlev law, also known as the anti-Magnitsky law, whereby Russia decided Americans could no longer adopt Russian babies. The law is described as a response to the Magnitsky Act in the United States that placed sanctions on Russian officials involved in a tax scandal exposed by Russian lawyer Sergei Magnitsky, who was purportedly tortured in prison. As a reminder, should it be lost in this shuffle, a child died here, and children who might need families will be bureaucratically blocked from helping them. But also, the first shot fired in a new Cold War.

HEDGING: A word window, purposefully left ajar, to allow an interpretive draft.[56]

---

[56] There was nobody looking over our shoulder telling us what we could and couldn't write, but nevertheless, every ad and article needed to be reviewed under the pretext of what could be allowed. Cartoonish video game ads were the steadiest offenders; most needed to be carefully edited for showing too much skin. I never saw a censor once, though I was repeatedly warned that if ever some older devout-looking men came to the door, we should not speak to them but make sure that the owner did. These vague threats just sort of hung out there.

Most of the time, you felt as if you were safe, and mostly you were. Though the locale was foreign, there was a Chili's, an Ikea, a Starbucks; movie theaters playing Western-style movies. With two-thirds of the population foreigners, and a significant amount of those American or British, it could easily seem that you were in a place similar to home. That you had the same rights as at home. I did not have the same rights as at home and was perhaps just too careless to have noticed.

The *wasta* system too, which assured that locals were favored over foreigners, had a chilling effect on an everyday societal level. A local could drive down the freeway going 140 mph without any fear of police, and often did. They would drive at full speed in the space on the freeway between lanes. Or perhaps in the store, someone would cut in line in front of twenty people and there was nothing you could say. You were a foreigner, and sometimes they made you know it. But these were merely inconveniences, not even worth mentioning compared to the troubles that many other foreigners faced in the country.

HELL-BENT: You mean focused and goal-oriented?[57]

---

[57] The job was wonderful even with the restrictions on content. We operated as a casual multinational team, constantly with the pressure of deadlines in the background. I went everywhere in the city and we were special guests at all of the big events in town. My writing assignments ranged from food reviews to an interview with a female Kuwaiti veterinarian to the opening of the latest section of the mall.

Once I interviewed a guy who had come to town on a Red Bull–sponsored event to be the first person to BASE jump in Kuwait; he was to do so off the highest building in the country. We met in the lobby of the building, a posh spot. Had coffee. Did the interview. Then, for color, a photographer and I were to accompany him to the roof for a sort of preview. Shots before the jump. We went up to the roof in a group of about ten of us: the jumper, security, a few people from the PR team, the photographer, and me.

The first seventy floors or so could be taken by elevator, then we had to use the stairs. When we got off the elevator, we were shocked to see that that several of the top floors were simply unfinished inside. Building tools everywhere. We got to the roof expecting a deck of some sort but were surprised to find a rather precarious footing. Because the building was designed to look like the sail of a Kuwaiti dhow, there was no flat roof to speak of. Just an oversized window-washing rig to try to move around on and a few odd spots where you could stand, eight floors up with no railing. We watched the jumper plan his route: where he could run from, how he might flip off, why—due to dangers of the wind—he couldn't just fly loops around the building on the way down as the event organizers were requesting.

So, it was exciting, and every day was different. I loved my coworkers as much as I loved our little spats about content. We argued, too, about commas. Someone had to explain to me what the word bespoke meant. But between these I got to write all kinds of content that was just fun: music reviews and culture critique, always with a Western spin. Things that to me were in line with the weeklies I'd grown up idolizing, even if there were limits to what we could write.

But I also knew that it couldn't last. That I was not going to stay there forever. I had plans. I couldn't say for sure what they were, but I knew they involved writing and that I would need to learn more than I could where I was.

HELL-FOR-LEATHER: Faster than fast.[58]

---

58 It was still dark when I got into my car to go to work. A year in now, I'd been leaving increasingly earlier in order to avoid the frustrations of morning traffic. I'd learned, too, the various shortcuts through the desert to get to the freeway, first via the hole in the fence, later over curbs and parking lots; by following the lead of the locals I could shave off half an hour easy. Once on the highway I'd hum along in the dark. I usually used the Sixty to Fourth Ring Road to drive around Kuwait City proper, but this day, due to some bottleneck I went on to the Third Ring instead, further toward the city center. Though the speed of travel remained high, the road itself was just two lanes in each direction. I followed an SUV a little too close in the fast lane at approximately 70 mph—I think, because my car read in kph—hoping the driver might move over. Another car had matched my speed to my immediate right, albeit slightly behind, when the SUV in front of me suddenly whipped right, fishtailed heavily and precariously back and forth before recovering a moment later, a full lane over. It simultaneously revealed its reason for doing so: a large square vehicle stopped in the fast lane.

In an instant I made the decision not to swerve into the car on my right, but instead to slam on the brakes and brace for impact, to take the hit. And even as the wheels locked up and I began to skid forward in slow motion, and the car beside me sped off into a dark nearly but not quite fecund with dawn, I thought I knew that I'd possibly perhaps braked from far enough away that I would not die. That this was the better decision. Mid-slide, as I approached what appeared to be a street-sweeper with no hazard lights or indicators coming into focus, my tires painted a black rubber squiggle on the highway. There was no movement anywhere near the vehicle and no one in it, I hoped, while increasingly worried about the shape of the oversized machine's broad back, clearly made of sturdy steel, with a high bumper that was about at windshield height. But I still thought I might be fine.

And I was fine.

Shook up, but fine. The car was accordioned, the front license plate seemingly touching the dashboard. The airbag deployed and there was dust everywhere. The car's front axle sat on the ground, its wheels seemingly folded into metal. Fluids spilled. It was at the very least, not drivable. There was no one around. No one in the street-sweeper. No cars stopping, only an increasing amount of traffic as I stood there trying to figure what to do. Sarah was at work so I texted her and told her I was okay. I reached out to my boss at the magazine, sure he'd know what to do. The phone rang several rings too long before he answered with a question to the tone of his hello, likely because of the time. I spit it out: I think I'm okay. The other driver isn't here. What do I do? *Wait for the police. Get a translator if you can.* I paced back to the small island on the center curb, cars racing past. After a couple of too-close calls, I walked further away from the car to warn oncoming drivers of the danger ahead by waving a hand. The sun was just beginning to rise. An Indian worker in a full yellow jumpsuit arrived and regarded the accident from the other side of the road. He put his head in his hands at the sight of me, then pulled a cell phone from his pocket, gesticulating wildly to whomever was on the other end. After a minute, he hung up the phone and crossed onto the center median. People honked their frustrations at us while we waited.

I called Anwar, a local taxi driver whom we sometimes used at the compound and asked if I could hire him as a translator for the morning. He agreed, warning me that they would require me to go to a local police station. Told me to call him when I knew where. A police car pulled up. Two officers got out. One stood next to the car and lit a cigarette. The other made his way across traffic to the center median and began inspecting the cars. When he realized I didn't speak Arabic he stopped trying to communicate with me altogether and waved the other officer over to discuss the finer points of the scene. The street-sweeping vehicle, with its tanklike construction and bumper that could have graced a military-grade vehicle, appeared to have suffered no damage all. After another hour a tow truck showed up. They pulled my car onto a flatbed, instructed that I should get in, and we headed to what I hoped was the police station. It was, and Anwar was waiting for me there. I greeted him like he was my only friend in the world because at the time, he felt like it.

Things happened rather quickly after that. We were to appear before a judge, and the proceedings would all be in Arabic. The street-sweeper was owned by the state, I was told, and their contention was that the accident was all my fault. The seriousness of my situation struck me then: it was me against the state, and Anwar was the closest thing I had to a lawyer.

HERD MENTALITY: Conforming.[59]

HIKIKOMORI: Those who shut themselves in online and withdraw from material society in favor of a digital one.

HIPSTER: A twenty-first-century urban male with the fashion sensibilities of an eighteenth-century rural one.

[59] The first time I went to Dubai, it was to cheer up a friend who'd moved there to be with a girl who broke up with him shortly after he arrived. He was stuck there in a contract he couldn't get out of. She'd left town with someone else. He was depressed.

Because my friend was the type who didn't plan, I wasn't surprised at all that he was not at the airport when I arrived. I waited, bag in hand, standing by a pillar near what seemed to be a pick-up zone. A minute or two in, a young man, seemingly American, stopped next to me to smoke, dropped his rucksack. He mentioned something about the heat, the flight. Small talk. A few minutes later another man approached. Then a woman. Then a few more men. I assumed they were military because they wore the unofficial uniform: hair cropped close, beefy builds, a few too many tattoos for this part of the world. Soon all of the semi-matching bags confirmed my theory. Before long, the group had grown large enough that I stopped noticing when people arrived, though they were all conspicuously American. Then a bus pulled up not too far away and they all piled on.

Hey bro—you coming? the guy who'd been talking to me asked, hanging halfway out the bus door.

Not my ride, I replied.

Oh, we just assumed.

This was seemingly the only prism in which me being in the Middle East made sense to anyone. Or maybe I just happened to be standing in a signless GI pick-up zone? Or more likely, simply because I wore the same unofficial uniform that I spotted on them. It's possible.

HOBSON'S CHOICE: No choice at all. **SEE ALSO:** ***THE ILLUSION OF CHOICE***.[60]

[61]

HOSTILE ATTRIBUTION BIAS: The world is, in fact, out to get you. Plan accordingly.

---

[60] In a makeshift court, with my sometimes taxi driver representing me as my translator cum lawyer, the judges looked on as Anwar explained what my options were.

I could stay in the country and fight to get the owner of the street-sweeper, who incidentally was The State, to pay damages on my car because they'd left a broken-down vehicle in the fast lane of a freeway at night with no hazards or other warnings. But I should know that The State would plan to drag the proceedings out as long as they could *because* they could, which would likely mean a period of three to five years, but one never knows. And while any case is pending, of course, I would not be allowed to leave the country for any reason. Of course.

Or

I could walk away, me taking responsibility for the damage to my my own vehicle and The State doing the same, and the incident would be considered concluded.

The choice, he said they said, was mine.

[61] In our continued efforts to best illustrate the general tenor of the country at this time, *Hope* has been removed from the 2020 edition of this dictionary.

HOUSE OF CARDS: Insufficient material for dwelling construction. Also not recommended: lies, glass, or mirrors. Other than that, it's wide open.

HUMAN ERROR: Inevitable.

HYPERBOLE: Preferable.

HYPER OBJECT: Imperceptible.

HYPERSENSITIVE: Probable.[62]

---

[62] The end of Sarah's contract loomed in the distance. We would have to make a decision soon. She loved her students and her friends but found the politics of international teaching somehow even worse than in the States. It would be her last stint in the classroom. For me, I loved my work and my coworkers, but knew that it was only a step to the next thing. I applied to schools from California to New York, focusing on what I thought was the best state-school option and the best private one. West Coast or East? To know what I chose you'll need to know things about my psyche that I suspect I didn't even know myself.

In the back of my mind was a preference for New York City, but it was a problem that I had no SAT scores. Years out of school—why would I? I'd missed the closest test in the region—Dubai—and there wasn't enough time before the application deadlines to get the exams done for the next school year. The next closest regional test was in western Europe, but it was past the necessary date anyway. The fine print on the school's website indicated a test you could take instead if you showed up on campus and completed it in person. It felt like a dare.

It was 6,344 miles away, thirteen hours and fifty minutes direct, though more likely eighteen-plus hours and a layover in Germany. It would cost $3,000 and four days. I could make that work with my schedule at the magazine if I added a day of work to the weeks on either side. My wife says I asked her what she thought in a way that suggested I already knew what I was going to do, that she can tell this by a look I get. For what it's worth, though, she agreed that I should try.

I arrived in New York City a few weeks later and spent the night in Chinatown, on the couch of a friend who'd moved there at least in part to hide from a California warrant. *You're here for what, exactly?* he asked when I showed up on his stoop.

Like him, you may need me to explain the gumption.

You'd likely first have to know that years earlier I'd dropped out of Bible College and community college both, in that order, feeling like I didn't belong at either, though my own mother had recently gone back to college. She was eighteen when I, her third child, was born, and wherever my father was, he hadn't passed seventh grade. His parents were migrant farmworkers. My stepfather was imprisoned for an extended period of years for actions taken in his role as the regional president of what the state and federal governments called an "International Outlaw Biker Gang"—or, perhaps more comically, OMG's—but we just called "The Club."

When I met my wife, she'd already earned a master's degree. I can't be sure that she was the first person I'd ever known with one, but it couldn't be far off. Her father was a geophysicist who worked with former Eastern Bloc countries to establish nuclear-detection facilities at their borders, and her mom, who had a doctorate in French literature that she just didn't use, was part of the legal team for a large international oil company. You'd need to know that the term *married up* was very often hurled at me, but that I had no defense for when it was. The term itself had to be explained to me the first time I heard it.

I woke up early the next morning, got ready, and snuck out of my friend's cramped apartment, trying not to wake him. I hailed a cab like a tourist when the subway would have been faster. For nearly an hour, we inched our way up toward my firmly scheduled test: through Greenwich, SoHo, Chelsea, past Times Square, through Hell's Kitchen, me not even knowing enough yet to insist instead on the West Side Highway. Soon I would have cause to know.

I

IF YOU SEE SOMETHING, SAY SOMETHING *(PHRASE)*: Are you sure you want to convince an army of untrained civilians that it's their patriotic duty to police other people's actions?[63]

I HAVE MY MOUTH IN YOUR EARS *(PHRASE)*: My son takes to saying this one day, and it catches me off guard, something ominous and Machiavellian sounding in its construction, like a literal translation of an old Roman proverb. At any rate, after too many early mornings waking to find me working on this strange little book, he made me add this.

---

63 Whether by email, advert, or random interruption, Alexa wants me to know that, with the right add on, there's so much more she could be doing for me. But even in her hypothetical I read only the potential frustration: A neighbor stops by and Alexa answers the door. I've asked her to stop, but I might not be communicating in a way that works for her. She hears me, but fails to understand. Speaking through a system, she says that I'm not home. Neither is she, of course, and the friend knows this, which makes this whole exercise moot. She records the friend's door knocking so she can prove to me who it is. I don't have this, but my neighbor does. And if my neighbor does, should I? At what point is a little extra protection or convenience my own contribution to an entire surveillance state?

ILLEISM: It is indeed a sickness to talk about oneself in the third person, he thought as he typed this.[64]

IMMATURE: It seems certain that all technological progress will likely need to account for the fact that while boys will be boys, men will, too.[65]

---

64 Yet he fell into a research wormhole all the same, straining to avoid encyclopedic and compendium bumps along the way, nevertheless finding himself battered by the abundance of the archive: commercial, militaristic, theological, plastics, comic, acrostic, and a vast expanse of satirical commentary on societies past. What seemed, at first, original soon could only be perceived as the latest in a long line of abecedarian exploitation.

65 And we decided in Kuwait that it was time, maybe, to try to have kids. I wouldn't say I acquiesced as I don't think that's it at all. Something had changed. I'm not sure why exactly. I knew that in trying to write I had been dealing with a lot of my issues of childhood, but I didn't yet believe in the magic of it or anything. Not yet. I had to write and read much more before that could happen. I think, also, that all I ever knew of having children was that it was a sentence of some sort. A burden. That it meant your life was over. It was something that happened to everyone in my family, and they dealt with it because that's what you do.

But now, our lives were just starting to look more like something we wanted. I was working a job I actually loved with the possibility of more writing in the future, and we were approaching something like contentment. We weren't resigned to a life that we were sold; we were carving out our own. So, in that happiness, we started to try.

It would be wrong to say that I was certain, or without doubt, but it was a conscious choice that we both moved toward knowingly, and with great care, and that, for me—as much as anything else—was what I needed to enter fatherhood with.

IMPOSTER SYNDROME: The only thing worse: imposter syndrome imposters.[66]

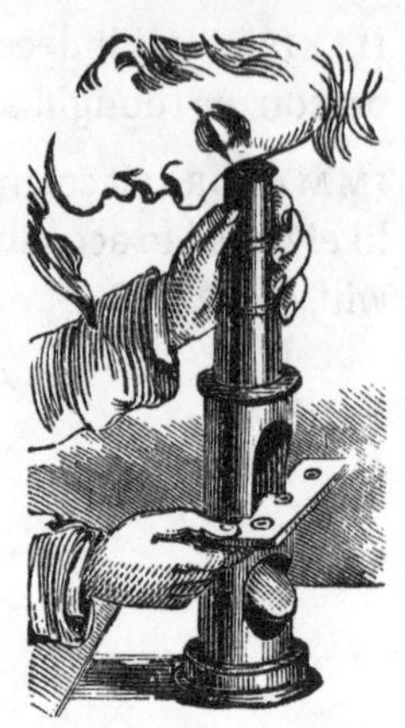

---

[66] In Kuwait, right about the time people would start to gather in large numbers in the square, another national holiday would be given, or citizens would get a direct deposit into their bank accounts. That's how it was explained to me anyways by the locals I knew. The next day, nobody was protesting in the square. It was remarkably effective. We knew better than to say, *This kind of thing would simply never happen in America.* And yet you feel it. It's lodged in the back of your throat, smug and unarticulated.

We decided to head to Bahrain for the weekend. Arab Spring was there too, oscillating between business as usual and anti-government flare-ups. These too became normalized because they came in waves. Incident, protest, resolve. Incident, protest, resolve.

Protest
Protest
Protest
(inciting) Incident
Resolve

Bahrain felt largely resolved at this point, judging by the news, but little more; they were in the midst of their own response in ways unseen on the surface. It was safe, but not completely so. My wife and several friends and I were looking forward to a brief weekend trip. On the quick flight over, we filled out our visa arrival cards. I was excited when it asked for occupation, wondering what word I should use. Am I a writer? Is that what I am now? I scolded myself: I mean, if you need to ask.

I settled on the word *journalist*, though this too felt ambitious. It was both true and not true. It is true that I was a staff writer for a national publication, but it just increasingly felt like advertorial, not that anyone else called it that. I turned the paper toward my wife in the seat next to me, as if to ask, Is this right? Is this what I am now? She nodded, proudly, and it felt like a very small arrival of sorts.

When we arrived, the teachers I traveled with moved through customs freely. I was separated and moved in another direction. I saw my friends traveling away from me down a very long corridor, my wife occasionally turning her body completely back, unsure which way she was in fact supposed to be going. Was she with me or with them? *With them*, I said with my wave.

I was immediately detained in a room by myself. After a while a group of men in military uniforms and fatigues entered and took turns speaking to me in hurried Arabic. I couldn't tell if they were actually yelling or it was just the different tonal expressions of another language. I was so naïve I had not considered the repercussions of being an American journalist with multiple questionable stamps on his passport. Blind to the consideration that they might not want Western eyes peeking in at their struggle. And unsure where my friends or my passport or my belongings or my gumption to call myself a journalist had suddenly gone.

At some point it became clear to me in the conversation that they didn't believe me. They thought, by looking at me, that I didn't look like a journalist, that I was likely military or something similar. It would have been silly to be offended—I could see it too, as did the soldiers in Dubai.

INATTENTION, CIVIL: To see something and *not* say something. We ignore each other in public to give each other privacy when we assume that we are not in danger. This poses a problem when breached.

INDOCTRINATION: The Grand Plan first tabled at the Secret Professor Society Meeting of 1754, where it was determined that the best way to brainwash young adults was to teach free-thinking strategies, welcome dissent, and arm them with the skills to decipher complex rhetorical practices.

INFILTRATOR: A recurring theme throughout the history of all literature is this: where are you from and who is your father? To know you, to know if you are one of us or one of them, we must be able to answer this question. But what if we can't answer so easily? Do we remain outsiders?[67]

---

[67] I was never mistreated by the Bahraini police, though intimidation seemed the point. Several guards, each one increasingly high ranking, came into the small room, something between an interrogation room and an office. It quickly became obvious that I needed to sell them the idea that, though I was an American and a journalist, I was in no way a threat. I wasn't there to report on their ongoing domestic problems related to Arab Spring. And just in case they were making the same assumptions some tended to, I definitely was not a soldier, either.

I fell rather easily into belittling my own work: the tea-length skirt and fashion articles, the food reviews about places I didn't even like, puff pieces on local businesses I had not even necessarily visited. When this proved to be working, but not entirely sufficient, I moved toward declaring myself a student more than anything, Columbia University in New York City, in fact, and university officials would be concerned if I wasn't available when they tried to reach me. (My admittance letter was still fresh in my pocket metaphorically, at least.) This last one seemed to help, though that may be my imagination. I thought I felt for the first time the value of a name-brand education.

And I wasn't even a student yet.

I was released after a couple of hours.

Over the course of the weekend, there were several times when I had the feeling my group was being followed. This likely wasn't even paranoia so much as standard practice, if they legitimately thought I was a journalist there to report on their governmental instability. Still, being paranoid about being paranoid was part of the psychic stress. I can't explain it, and it's crazy to try, but maybe a face was seen too often, a person idling too long in the vicinity while you're shopping. There were signs I would not be so bold as to call signs.

INFORMATION ASYMMETRY: A lower hand coinage if ever there was one.[68]

INSTITUTIONAL TRUST, EROSION OF: A ship that's sailed.

INSURANCE: We insure to ensure a certain sureness in our daily life when the only actual assurance is the common lack of surety had by most that the organization will do so.[69]

IT IS WHAT IT IS *(PHRASE)*: But if it's said often enough, it's something else.

[68] Offensive things said to me during my time among the Business Elite, Volume 1:

> You know when we knew we had China by the balls? When they started using toilet paper. That's it. They're hooked.
>
> We need someone of your, uh, *stature*, to work the East LA & Compton territory. You'll feel more at home there.

Sounds like someone's mother was a bit of a hussy.

No bonuses this year, but we've decided we're going to take you shopping for appropriate clothes.

We need someone of your, uh, *disposition*, to work the new Hispanic cleaning booth at the conference.

Someone like you . . . (∞).

[69] I put little effort into anything.

NOT AT ALL SLIGHTLY SOMEWHAT A LOT

J

JADED: Not the act of being pelted with a green mineral stone, but should it happen, having already anticipated it and let the world know, you'd have expected no less.[70]

JARGON: Language so *siloed* as to be useful only in narrow context. SEE ALSO: *SILOED*.[71]

JUGGERNAUT: An overwhelming force that can't be untied.

JUNKET: An insider meeting to sell a movie. Sometimes a recommendation as to what to do with the movie itself, after said meeting.

JUNK MAIL: Where one traditionally found correspondence from loved ones, one now finds only commerce, potential for future or receipts from previous.

---

70 After only a few months of trying to conceive, Sarah is convinced something is wrong. Nothing is happening, she says, but it doesn't seem to me that we've even really been trying yet. Kind of, but not really. Not to the point that it would seem something must be wrong, anyway. I can't tell if saying so encourages or discourages her. But at the heart of this is something she is not yet able to articulate. She thinks something is wrong with her. This is a weight she lives with. This fear. I come to see it slowly. We're trying. We vow to try more aggressively. Let's try for reals now, I say, and for reals we do.

71 The language of Johnson's definitions is not my own: that which, the state of being, the art of, to act upon, in an X manner, a machine which, he who has, a word noting, a species that, a passage where . . .

JUSTIFICATION: The heart of the feeling that is making us act terrible to each other, often hidden in the place where you should find shame

or regret
or kindness
or empathy
or disappointment
or repentance
or apology
or dismay
or penitence
or guilt
or compunction
or self-reproach
or . . . [72]

[72] . . . sympathy or help or Jesus or faith or a mirror or culpability or honest assessment or necessary giving or willingness to help or ability to give even when you won't get anything for it or feelings of altruism or the golden rule or whatever else you want to call it. Instead, justified.

KAINOTOPHOBIA: A fear of the new, like this spelling of cainotophobia.[73]

KAREN: The generic name for white woman, aggrieved. To not see the long history of how this trend of assigning a generic name as representative of all within a culture has been used against people of color and notice only, instead, your desire to not be stereotyped as such, is *peak*-Karen behavior.

KERFUFFLE: Agree to disagree, but with fists.[74]

---

73 I approach life with intensity.

NOT AT ALL SLIGHTLY SOMEWHAT A LOT

74 On November 24, 2013, network TV aired the 216th episode of the animated TV show *Family Guy*, in which one of the main characters, Brian, the dog, was killed; complicating this was the fact that another character, Stewie, had recently broken his time machine. So even though Brian had previously died once before, and come back, this time looked final. Within hours, a Change.org petition started up, asking the writers to bring him back. Not one to miss a cultural moment—the shows were aired on cable network OSN in Kuwait—I convinced the owner to let me write a full-page *New York Times*–style obituary for Brian on the inside back cover of the magazine.

KICKSTARTER: How an increasing percentage pay for either health insurance or the costs associated with dying; fundraising as a matter of normal practice due to societal disparities.[75]

KINESTHETIC LEARNING: I must touch it to learn it.[76]

---

75 In 2017, a New Jersey woman starts a GoFundMe campaign for a selfless, homeless veteran who helped her by giving her his last $20 when she ran out of gas. She and her boyfriend want to raise $10,000 to help get him off the street. It would be tough to guess exactly what people are responding to, but we could try: the selflessness of the man, yes. The last of his money, the size of the ask, the fact that he is a veteran.

It works too well: the post goes viral and a total of 14,347 people end up donating a total of $402,706. The money goes to the couple who set up the post, of course. They set up a bank account for the homeless man, Johnny Bobbitt, but place only $25,000 in it. They justify this by saying they don't want him to blow it, despite that being exactly what they do over the next year: on gambling, expensive trips, high-end clothing, and luxury handbags. They buy a camper, too, and place it on their property for the homeless guy, who does live there for a short time.

It takes over two years for the full story to unravel, and only because, as in all great heists, the protagonists end up arguing over their cut of the money and Bobbitt sues the couple, Katelyn McClure and her boyfriend Mark D'Amico. Apparently, all three plotted to create a fake feel-good story to trick people into donating. Police end up finding a total of 60,000 text messages between the accused parties about the case, including a text Ms. McClure sent to a friend in the hour after the campaign started. When her friend tries to parse which parts of the narrative are true, Ms. McClure responds, "I had to make something up so people feel bad."

76 We ask Alexa to set a reminder at 5 p.m. every day to feed the dog. My son revels in setting it up. He still has his jokes with her and is excited for what at first seems to be a game. They are getting closer, I think—like, friends, maybe—and then I correct myself for the thought. They can't be friends; she's not real. But she's real to him. It's his first official daily chore, and for a while, he's happy to have the role. Soon though, a change. "This is your reminder: Feed the dog." What is at first an enthusiastic jump-up response is soon reduced to an audible and drawn-out "Ahhhhh" pitching first upward, and then downward in exasperation. The thing is, he's not mad at us for having to do it; he's mad at her.

KISMET: A book, a town, a robot, a mindset. A global to-do list. A belief offering the same comfort to a believer as a god might.[77]

KOMPROMAT: How it started.[78]

---

[77] The January issue was the last I wrote in-country. At the Kuwait airport, as I left to start again in a new city, I saw issues on newsstands and felt proud. One of the last articles I wrote was a rebirth announcement for Brian after the TV show found a loophole to bring him back, as expected. It too, was meant to look official. I'd pitched it as the magazine's obligation to respond. I had a fully envisioned idea, with a stained-glass picture of Brian's head on a stained-glass body. I was more invested in the art than the article by that point. Even though I didn't pick the specific picture, I'd guided the religious iconography. I insisted, prevailed, and was proud of how it came out.

[78] How it's going: 

L

LACKADAISICAL: Slander, I say.[79]

---

79 If I wasn't the laziest child born inside of three counties, I was undoubtedly a contender. Nobody had to tell me so—I just knew it. I was always looking for an angle to make things easy, a way to get out of work or maybe even make a buck. I was the only one of five siblings—a number that changes over the years, but herein includes whole, though not all, and step—ever to be put on permanent restriction from chores for doing them wrong; it was I who received the Pizza Hut Book It! award for most books read in all of the third grade without glimpsing so much as the first and last pages, just so I could get the free pizza; and I was the kid in my thousand-unit apartment complex known for charging other kids a quarter to play makeshift carnival games for the chance to win my older brother's stuffed animals. I needed snack money. There was ingenuity to it, but I suspected laziness at its core. Hunger too, apparently.

At some point, I decided I was lazy because I had no dad around, but that logic quickly proved spurious, as my mom—like most of the women in my family—was stricter than any men I'd ever met. Still, the consensus on my block was that I was a half-hazard, laurel-resting, lazy-bones jones. I decided then and there that nobody was gonna call me half a nothin' and get away with it, never mind that I was apparently a lazy listener, too. The misheard word internalized—and not for the last time.

I don't recall when I first heard the word *lackadaisical*, but I remember thinking it was as pointed and sharp as it was confusing. Not a word so much as a phrase whose constituent parts defied an easy read, a Germanic *stackability* to its composition. It sounded like a cry, giving way to a quality—a lifestyle, even. But was it a lack of *days* or a lack of *daze* that I exuded? Was it time or bewilderment that was diminishing? The word obscured, but it felt like an accusation all the same.

In Shakespeare's *Romeo and Juliet*, when Romeo stumbles into the church and onto Juliet's dead body, he cries, "She's dead. Alack the day." This is the earliest known use of the phrase. Something has died, but something, too, is born. Through a glacial semantic drift, the phrase changes:

alacktheday → lacktheday → lackadaisy → lackadaisical

The word was a statement, pushed and pushed on until it became another thing entirely. I feel that. Time, pressure, repetition, a process of etymological erosion called *aphesis* that slowly rounds out extraneous vowel edges, making a tight whole of all its requisite parts.

In the years I caught religion, I thought I could solve the father thing and laziness at the same time. The church made remarkably efficient work of sensing vulnerability in kids and sliding in as equal parts trusted friend and firm parent. The good book was all rules and structure, and every teen social event had its dry, church-sponsored equivalent. I threw myself into it so hard, I woke up in a Canadian Bible College at eighteen just begging god to explain himself for what increasingly seemed unresolvable discrepancies.

LEGALESE: To catch a case of Lawyermouth.[80]

LEGALISTIC: For a while, I could only conceive of a very literal Jesus. I didn't realize I was trying to fill the hole of father with father, even if he was also a son. I craved rules, structure, and that's what the Bible was.[81]

---

80 Plausible deniability of mutual self-interest heretofore and in perpetuity referred to as negligible.

81 If we were going to have rules, it seemed to me that they needed to be absolute, and the more involved I got with church, the more people seemed to bend god's words as they wished. I went from performing just about all manner of sins—precociously—to a boy who could not cross the street for fear of jaywalking since breaking man's law was breaking god's law on earth. Preacher said I was being legalistic, but I just took it seriously, that's all. To this day, when I hear people condemn jihadists, I have to quiet the part of me that, despite my disagreement and misgivings to say so, sees them as simply appropriately committed.

When god and I broke up, I was again untethered; the moral relativism that followed left me feeling more adrift than before. It seemed the only thing worse than no organizing principle to life was having one that had dissolved.

It has been years since I have been accused of anything approaching unfocused. I've been determined, dogged even. In that place where religion used to sit, I placed an ethic of work. It is an easy trap to fall into in America: work as religion. It was a willing stand-in for god and took up just as much time, too. I felt myself become, over time, that version of an American businessman who talked through people, saw only problems and responses, maximum yield, minimal loss. Cost/benefit ratios. Ends that cared not if the means were even justified at all. It took me years to see that I had overcorrected.

I have seen things crushed from being held too tight. Ideas wrung of all heart, leaving only the rind of what once was. Relationships folded under that pressure, friendships too. Friends could see in my lack of presence me planning my response or exit two steps ahead. I wasn't really present at all so much as powering through with my plan—*any* plan—as my North Star.

I suppose I found in planning what I had lost in religion. You simply can't have an existential crisis when you've got a to-do list on your person. I've been wondering lately if perhaps there is a halfway, though, between lackadaisical and its opposite. A plan that also plans for magic and, more importantly, makes time for it.

LIBERTIES: If they are inalienable, then they can only ever be taken from you, never given. And what about the connotation of taking liberties? To take liberties with someone or something, say, the truth.

LIFE COMPATIBILITY: Accidental acknowledgment that some things are not.[82]

LIFE HACKS: One person's life hack is another person's *the way*.[83]

---

82 Seeing a job through to the end is important to me.

NOT AT ALL SLIGHTLY SOMEWHAT A LOT

83 Alexa, play *Footloose*. Inspired by a recent showing of the movie on TV, this request, too, is a game that begins in earnest but quickly turns into a friendly, third-party antagonism, a spousal chiding that one should improve one's mood.

LIGHT POLLUTION: An absence creator. A magic trick for the skies wiping away celestial bodies—look at you, you're glowing and in your glowing, I am diminished next to you. Me and others too, that you can't see surround you. We are enveloped by your radiance. This is not the Great Pacific Garbage Patch, and this is not our widening belt of space debris, but it is, all the same, the byproduct of our daily living, some unquantified sheen we emit nightly.

LIMINAL: Everything is.[84]

---

[84] My plane had barely landed in New York when I received a text instructing me to check my voicemail, then voicemails to check my email. It was my boss back at the magazine. He sounded upset, frantic even. "Hey, man, we're in a bit of trouble over here. Give me a call when you get in. Later, man." The tone was ominous. The latter *man* hung there, conspicuous. One too many to be casual, suggested he was lifting something heavy.

I checked. There was a whole chain of email correspondence between him, some mediating agency, the magazine's lawyer, and a local Coptic Orthodox Christian Church—the largest and most wealthy Christian diocese in the Middle East. The emails indicated that an article I recently wrote had offended the church. I knew instantly which one they meant.

In all the time I spent there, what I feared most were the police and the invisible Muslim censors. As a journalist hired to push a more Western perspective during a time of social upheaval, I knew I was at some risk, but it didn't feel real. Still, it never occurred to me to fear the Christians—they weren't even on my radar. What blind assumptions. But I'd offended them, and was told that as far as they were concerned, heads were gonna roll. They demanded the writer be fired. They demanded the magazine shut down for good. They demanded an apology. This is exactly the type of legal action that gets your name on a list of people who can't get out of the country until the trial is over. My anonymity saved me, most likely.

The magazine survived by throwing me under the bus; I don't know that, but I can assume. There were some high-level *wasta* meetings and a public retraction that I helped them craft. *No, we do not, in fact, mean to liken Christ to a dog. Yes, we are quite sorry. That writer isn't even in the country anymore.* Still, I couldn't help but feel—in the uproar, in the danger even—like I might have found the journalism I was looking for: in the cartoon head of a dog, on Christ's body, as birth announcement. Something serious.

What worried us most was that Sarah was still in country. What helped us was that there was no name publicly attached to the article. There were records, too, that I'd left the country, no doubt. New city. No job. Pregnant wife in political danger in a Middle East nation. This was getting out of hand.

LIMITED HANGOUT: Spy-speak for a covert identity being blown and every get-together once you have children.[85]

---

[85] The choice was Sarah's: have the baby in Kuwait or New York City. There were logistical things to work out either way. I was heading to New York to prepare for our life there. Find a place and get us set up. I would start classes in spring, stay at a friend's house in Jersey City while I looked for a place for us in Manhattan's notoriously hard rental market. She would stay behind working, then on maternity leave until May, to finish her contract and wrap up the house there. The birth would cut close to the semester's end but the timetable was doable. I left Kuwait on New Year's Day.

For Sarah, there were ultimately more knowns in a birth in Kuwait City than in New York City: she liked her doctor there, an Egyptian man, American board certified, with an affable, though conservative, bedside manner. The hospital, too, was basically a spa: private rooms and chefs. The Royale Hyatt was the nicest in the country. In New York, by contrast, we didn't even know what borough we'd live in. We envisioned every middle-of-the-night ambulance ride through Manhattan we'd ever seen in a movie. The choice of having her baby with her friends beside her at a spa versus possibly on our own, in some unknown place, was an easy one. So her mom came out to live with us and help for the duration of the pregnancy. I was just a short flight away if needed. It wasn't a short flight, of course, it was two long ones and a layover, but nevertheless, this is how we sold it to ourselves.

Shortly after I'd left, we'd received a warning from the school liaison: while it was not *necessarily* a problem to be a pregnant foreigner, it was illegal to give birth there without the husband present. This meant that, at a certain point in the pregnancy, if I wasn't there, Sarah would be kicked out of the country. Though I planned to return for the birth, of course, we still needed paperwork to cover our circumstances so that I could quickly get there for the birth, pack us up, and return stateside, hopefully missing only a week of school.

It would be problem enough to get an okay to miss more than a class. Aside from acclimating to the pressures of university life—to say nothing of it being an Ivy, the low-level daily class warfare of it—I was an extended guest in someone's home, navigating a two-state commute each day and battling my first NYC winter. I spent the semester tangled in bureaucracy: drafting letters to the school, to the embassy, to local representatives in New York. Each document needed to be notarized, certified by a state representative, and its reciprocal process done on the receiving end (who knew a university would keep a notary on hand?). To get someone to issue my wife documents that were normally only issued to men took calling in favors, which could not be recorded as such, at the local embassy, with friends with *wasta* in Kuwait, and even with the school liaison herself, who, Sarah said, gave her the distinct impression she was only helping her because she thought she was pretty in a Western way. In the end, she was granted a provisional right to stay provided she agreed to leave the country within fifteen days of the child's birth. We promised.

LINGUA FRANCA: Whatever tongue is easiest. Whatever tongue can bridge us. Whatever the distance between you and me, this tongue. Give it to me. Meet me at the common ground.

LIQUEFACTION: A drunkard's propensity to speak the truth and something erroneously built. SEE ALSO: *HOUSE OF CARDS*.[86]

[86] A couple of professors said that they would work with me, no matter what, but as an undergrad in his first semester at a new school, I had neither the track record nor the bargaining power to overcome the ones who wouldn't. I would have to repeat the classes at a later date or take a temporary leave of absence or withdraw from the school if I had to leave or simply could not make their attendance policy work. Their reaction, I suspect, was caused by the implausibility of the situation, or perhaps just the sheer number of details that I didn't know—couldn't know—until they happened: the when and how long I would be gone. How many undergrads need to leave the country because their wives are giving birth, guaranteeing at least a week of missed classes? When our son's birth came, predictably, in the week or so before finals, we decided it was best that I not return. We couldn't afford, in either time or money, the total cost of me returning, then leaving, and eventually repeating a semester of name-brand education.

LISTICLE: Signs of a shortened attention span, and incidentally my primary assignment at my new *journalism* job in NYC.[87]

[87] TOP TEN REASONS YOU SHOULD NOT HAVE LEFT KUWAIT!

1. You left your wife behind.
2. She's pregnant.
3. In addition to being in poor taste, given the particularities, it's illegal.
4. You had a good writing job there, last of its kind.
5. School, at your age, is not a sensible decision.
6. Is this upward mobility or vanity?
7. The school is expensive.
8. New York City is expensive.
9. Journalism jobs don't pay much.
10. Doesn't leaving her behind make you just like your father?

LITERALLY: Often presented in opposition to figurative in a manner policing someone else's speech. Word-snobs—and regular snobs, too—like to suggest that *literal* was never also used as figurative, but this is literally not true.[88]

---

[88] One of my favorite word fights in recent years is the literal/figurative divide, primarily because it's one where people seem to have the most entrenched position, hardened, perhaps, by the logic that a word simply cannot have two meanings that contradict each other. Merriam-Webster currently defines literally as:

> in a literal sense or manner: actually
> in effect: virtually

In a usage note on Merriam-Webster online, a writer suggests that they've received a lot of heat for this and works hard to defend why they show the usage both ways by first noting that this is not a recent change. This matters because it's but one example people like to use to illustrate society's erosion, as they are sometimes wont to do. Citing authors from Charles Dickens and William Thackeray to F. Scott Fitzgerald, the blogpost shows a strong literary tendency for such hyperbole since at least 1769, before noting that their own dictionary has observed the use of literally figuratively since at least 1909.

One would be right, of course, to suggest that at the heart of this squabble are attitudes reflected in the difference between prescriptive and descriptive dictionaries—the former prescribing how language should work and the latter simply describing how it is working—but at the very least, it is not a sign of language devolving, of the English apocalypse that many make it out to be. We can argue over the benefits of prescriptive and descriptive approaches to language, though these days, scholars often see a benefit in both. They are tools approaching language from different directions that, pieced together, give a more accurate understanding of what the English language has done and is doing. Long live the hybrid!

So, at the very least, the next time someone tries to correct you, and tell you you're wrong for using literally in a figurative manner, they are taking a position that has been wrong, as of this writing, for literally 110 years.

LONG-STORY-SHORT: A conversational accelerator, theoretically, though this has not been my experience.[89]

LOOPHOLES: Exploitable possibilities normally discovered by lawyers, for those who can afford them.

---

[89] And that's how, when the time came, when our dog woke Sarah in the middle of the night to alert her that her water had broken, when she calmly got up and grabbed her bag and walked down the cold-tile hall to wake her mom in the next room, who in turn calmly readied herself and walked them both out to the elevator and down to the car, where they argued briefly about who would drive because her mom knew neither the shortcut to the highway nor the labyrinthine roads from Mahboula to Salmiya in the early predawn, when she pulled up to the hospital and was quickly checked in, I found myself in the kitchen of my friend's Jersey City apartment, cramming where the internet was strongest, by a window that refused to seal, a late snow still refusing to melt outside. Over a period of hours, I watched, from the frigid windowsill, the sun's rise through a sliver of view between three buildings. The idea to stream in to watch the birth of my son sounds terrible, felt terrible, and was worsened by the need for a last-minute C-section when labor went on too long. Too many hours had passed since Sarah's water had broken, which would be a problem for the baby. By phone and Skype, simultaneously, I spoke with the doctor who, due more to local laws than the drugs she was now on, needed the approval of the husband to proceed, to which I said, after briefly speaking to her mother simultaneously, and wondering how it was possible that I was placed as the responsible party for her health, as the internet connection wavered, while her mother waved the iPad awkwardly around the room to speak between people—*Of course, do it!* As if there were another option. Wondering what he was asking me for. Our son was born, otherwise without a hitch. I was in class later that morning, an adult in a sea of children, playing undergrad, trying to make up for lost time.

LOW-INFORMATION VOTERS: An equal vote regardless of time spent considering it? Maybe. Or maybe just a way for the wealthy to suggest that not everyone should have a vote to begin with.[90]

LOW RENT: The only thing I ever heard my mother pray for during my entire childhood. Also, what I see when looking at me through the eyes of my in-laws.[91]

---

90 Given gerrymandering, Electoral College, felony disenfranchisement laws: no, your vote is not equal anyway. Imagine speaking Democracy out of one side of your mouth, while needing—as an operational standard—to suppress it from the other. Grift as standard business practice.

91 I say New York City, but I was actually in Jersey City. Sixth borough, they liked to say, while bragging about its proximity to downtown Manhattan. *Closer than Brooklyn, anyway,* a preemptive defense for a New Yorker's dismissal of anything Jersey. A friend was nice enough to put me up while I was looking for a place in Manhattan, closer to school. The commute was rough: PATH station over to 34th, then walk over a block to catch the 1 or 2 or 3, depending on time. But for some reason unbeknownst to me, the train had a habit of stopping at 77th Street, especially in winter; the school was at 116th. The walk could take an hour from there, or I'd have to scramble for a cab. The snow could make it all so much worse.

It takes a whole semester to get used to school, to recognize all of the ways I might not quite be prepared. To stand out among my cohort, and not just because I was old enough to be their parent. To measure my life against theirs. How did I ever end up here? I am trying to acclimate to a life while maintaining connection to another one halfway around the world. But it's fabulous too—the city, of course, and also everyone at school, who have stellar résumés as well as big ideas and seemingly the talent to achieve them. I felt I had entered through some side door, and maybe my peers weren't even sure why I was there. But I was there and that was all that mattered.

M

MAGIC WORD, THE: Neither hocus pocus nor alakazam; for presto change-o, just ask nicely.

MANCAVE: The part of an American home where a man might act like a boy. I mean, more than he normally does. Historical predecessor is the *diwaniya*. **SEE ALSO: *SHE-SHED*.**[92]

MANDATORY ARBITRATION: You only have to agree to this if you want the job. So . . .

MANSPLAIN: Well, I'm certainly not going to try to tell you.

MANSPREAD: In the animal world, deimatic behavior is any bluffing behavior wherein an animal seeks to make itself appear bigger than it is, often due to a lack of strong defenses **AKA THE *SUBWAY SLOUCH* OR *STARTLE DISPLAY*.**[93]

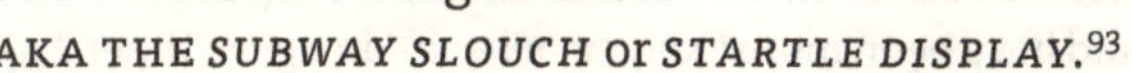

MANUFACTURED OUTRAGE: Coming down the assembly line.

---

92 I spend time doing things that interest me.

NOT AT ALL	SLIGHTLY	SOMEWHAT	A LOT

93 Can framing this in an emasculating way be the best way to curb the behavior?

MASCULINITY: So fragile as to become enraged when you say so. **SEE ALSO:** ***PRECARIOUS MANHOOD.***[94]

---

94 I wouldn't have known to use the word *shame*. Because Sarah and I were good with our decisions around our son's birth, had talked about it, worst-case-scenario-ed it—something I am prone to that actually drives her a bit nuts—I never much considered what the situation might look like to an outside observer. But I've wondered, in the years after, if my mother-in-law might have had any doubts that I would be there to meet them. I wondered, when my wife let it slip later that maybe a few friends questioned my not being at the birth of our child, had said some rather horrible things to her, how it might have looked from the outside. I wondered about the burden on Sarah.

I have to believe that Sarah didn't wonder if I'd be there at the airport, but could she have? As a boy whose father abandoned him, it would be hard for me to overstate what a central operating position that is. She would have been more likely to believe, I imagine, that I'd swoop through to pick up our son and forget my wife was even there, rather than not show at all. That was just simply something that was not in me to do. What I mean is, I can imagine all kinds of reasons why a couple—why a relationship—might not work out, but none that would keep a parent from a child. This is oversimplification, of course, but is also feels true to me.

So, it is on the one hand a great shame to me that I wasn't there, and on the other, not of consequence at all, particularly when compared to every day since. In conversations about my son's birth, though, I still dread this part. I justify. I am ashamed, in some way. And him having my name too, my exact name, was designed to signify in the official paperwork that this child belonged, that he was his father's son. That this child would be spoken for. And also vow to my son, too, that his father could never—would never—deny him, as mine did me. Does me.

MASS SHOOTING: Ten per week, every week, as of this writing. Perhaps we should go ahead and make the Active Shooter Kit the New American Backpack.

MEET-CUTE: A beginning, and sometimes the beginning of other endings.[95]

---

95 And then, a few weeks later, I met my son for the first time at the international arrivals gate at JFK, an oversized car double-parked out front to haul all of our belongings. As Sarah came down the escalator, a bundle in her arms and her mom behind her, she searched the crowd for me. I moved my way to the front as she stepped off. She collapsed into my arms and handed the baby to me in noticeable relief. She had not let on how hard it had been.

The boy was a peanut. Scrunched-up and sour faced, but otherwise calm. He'd traveled well, apparently only crying once. A flight attendant gave him wings. We didn't yet know that he'd been saving up his distress for the arrival stateside. I couldn't tell you who started crying first, but soon we all were. Enough that we were causing a scene even as we went about gathering up all of the bags, some actual bags, some duct-taped parcels of the international sort. My wife's mom gave us kisses, took pictures, cried some more, and scurried off to catch a flight back home to Denver. I got everything into the back of the car, and Sarah sighed a heavy sigh in the front seat, falling asleep almost immediately.

MENDEZ V. WESTMINSTER: Case precedent for *Brown v. Board*, which took place eleven miles from my hometown. The Vidaurri kids could stay; the Mendez kids must go, because what a last name and skin tone indexes, both in the eyes of the beholder, matters, arbitrary though it is.[96]

---

96 If you are looking for context clues, my name is a broken index. Each part a nominal incongruence. Don't you know brands suffer in ambiguity? My patrilineal name is—no, I must resist the urge to prove it to you. To give his name is to make a claim, just as it is not to. A double bind. I never took my father's name, and he never gave it. Among my siblings, skin tone, too, fluctuates wildly. Broken index. Among my father's siblings it's the same. And when I meet my grandmother on what will soon be her deathbed, she leans in and says breathily in a thick Mexican American accent, *Mijo they sometimes called me güera*, because she too had light eyes. Technically, Mexicans were considered white in America, due to a clause in the 1848 Treaty of Hidalgo, but then other white Americans decided otherwise. They can decide otherwise for you when they want to. Even now, if doing genealogical work, I can't read my ancestors' immigration cards without wondering if signifying white was a cover or an honest self-identification. That race is sometimes a screen on which others might play the movie they desire, casting you where they wish. At times, it's non-consideration, at others, they won't let you sign up for school.

One doesn't simply imagine these ghosts of racial reckoning, raising the hairs on the arm and neck; you perceive it. What the police meant when they said, *You're too ugly to be from around here*, the first time my brother and I got kicked out of Huntington Beach. I must have been about twelve. It was either race or the punk thing, mohawks and patched jackets. It's hard to tell, which is where the insidiousness lies. Still, it simply wasn't that long ago. Not that long since the Mendez mixed kids, just a few miles down the road. Not that long since the Orange Theater required Mexicans to sit in the balcony, not that long since the Hart Park pool had Mexican day on Mondays, the day before it was cleaned. That park where my brother and I swam as children; that theater, converted into a church where I was at one point saved and in front of which my brother was later nearly shot. His friends were, but he escaped, hurrying them all off to the hospital. And the Cypress Street school, the segregated school for Mexican kids in the Cypress barrio, just seven hundred feet away from my house, didn't close until three years after the Mendez case, making it one of the last segregated public schools in Southern California. These histories, tied to place, the ghosts we walk among.

MERCH: There are two options in America: Hustle or Hustle. A type of doing or a type of being.The choice is yours. If you're not selling something, are you even American?

METACOGNITION: Thinking about thinking about it.

METADATA: Digital detritus, too, can create narrative.[97]

---

97 We found a place on the corner of 122nd and Amsterdam through Columbia housing. The area was perfect, just between two parks. In the previous iteration of myself, I had worked hard to make money, which bought me time. Now I had no time because I had no money. Tracing data at the time would show: class, library, job 1, job 2, class, library, job 3, class, library. Job 1 was still writing for the magazine, but from afar. Job 2 was interning at a fast-paced news organization, job 3 was waiting tables at the restaurant downstairs from our place, then there was school, then fatherhood, then marriage. It was a lot, but we were making it work.

I'm told that my grandfather back in California is going to pass soon. I have a choice: see him before he dies or go to his funeral. I choose the first option and fly back between classes to spend one last time with him at his senior living facility. I take him out for ice cream. He gives me a book on the Dead Sea Scrolls, still wants to know why I dropped out of Bible College two decades before. He's saying goodbye and wants one last try at getting my soul right, presumably. I feel blessed to have this last chance with him. But later, when I do in fact miss his funeral, it still feels terrible. Like I'm just not present for family.

Working for a news organization on 5th Avenue in Manhattan was not without its charms. I felt, in a way, like I was doing the people's business. I was walking with the crowd, for once, through the hustle, to what felt like work at the center of the world. Have you ever had a job like that? I hadn't. At least, it felt that way at first.

Slowly it became obvious: not news—listicles. Gossip. The truth was, the biggest news we ever got to in my time there, in my department anyway, was the Sony hack, where new dirt was coming out about celebrities every few hours. I watched my higher-ups salivating over it, pulling the all-night hours to get often salacious information out there. *They've leaked the salaries of the CEO! They're going to release a new movie for free! Did you hear what Sony execs said about Adam Sandler?* It was entertaining, but it didn't feel like journalism. In fact, these weren't even the stories I was working on. I was tasked with making listicles about the latest child stars or the like while these stories were reserved for the executive editors.

Two things become quite clear: the pay and the speed. There was simply no money in it. Any idea I had of being able to sustain a life or a family that way seemed far-fetched. And the speed with which the modern newsroom needed to crank things out felt fraught with danger. You had to turn in several articles a day without much time for vetting, fact checking. It seemed that since everything could just go in, to be edited as you went along if it was wrong, there was no pressure—or interest—in getting it right the first time. The speed of the process worried me.

Nothing marked my end here so clearly for me as when a new person came on after me and quickly started excelling. What mattered wasn't that she was half my age, already a university graduate, and very quickly eclipsed me at work. She was the new star of our department. I was the straggler. What got to me was that she loved the work, and I could see that her love for it was tied to her success. There was no getting around it—I didn't love it. Not even close. Not in this iteration. She loved listicles. Bled them freely. Excelled at stuff that I did only because someone was forcing me to. I left shortly thereafter to focus my efforts on waiting tables.

MICROAGGRESSION: My initial want is to cite how these are only meaningful in the absence of macroaggressions, as if to minimize them, as if to say, I'm on fire over here and you're talking to me about smoke. I suspect this reaction is common among those for whom aggression in its more traditionally understood forms has been common. But aren't microaggressions so insidious because they come when you least expect them, when your guard is down, like a sneak attack? Doesn't their cumulative effect render great internal damage in the process? Smoke, too, kills. And it's not one or the other. Both can be true.

MICROHOTEL: How do I microhotel with an increasingly macrobody?

MICROSLEEP: Because who's got the time.

MILLENNIA: A yardstick by which to measure humanity, each with decidedly different concerns. What will be the defining characteristic of ours, I wonder?[98]

[98] This is the mark of the new millennium, though we were warned in the last: changes in the way we inhabit the planet make the emergence of new diseases inevitable. In 2002, SARS becomes the first pandemic of the new millennium when 8,100 people are infected across twenty-nine countries. 774 people die and it's tragic. Then, bird flu swine flu MERS Ebola Zika. In that order.

MINIMUM WAGE: The minimum amount they can pay the lower rungs of the proletariat not to revolt.[99]

---

99 When I graduate, Columbia gives us about a week to move out, supposedly an anomaly of graduating after a fall semester. We find a sublet on Craigslist. The deal sounds shady, but we don't have many options. The place turns out to be the fanciest place I've ever lived in: indoor pool, game room, door guy, and an elevated outdoor deck that stares directly down 34th Street from across the water. Oh, yeah, it's in Weehawken, New Jersey, just under the cliff where Aaron Burr and Alexander Hamilton had their duel. We'll be here eight months, while I'm waiting for an answer on grad schools. It's a gorgeous and idyllic in-between time.

My son runs into the marble bar at top speed. His face is split open just above the eye. It's his first major trauma. Thank god it's not the eye, we think, as he wails. Because it's Sunday morning, the squad at the local hospital is something like the B team. He gets stitches. We get home and fight to keep him awake for the prescribed amount of time for head trauma.

This doesn't look right, I say to my wife, after about an hour of being home. His stitches. What do you mean? she asks. There's not enough of them, I say. I've had a lot of stitches over the years, which of course doesn't make me an expert, but it certainly gives me opinions. We need to do something, I say, or that's going to be a major scar. We reach out to his pediatrician to see if we should stop by. She's in Harlem, which is now a ferry and two trains away. Plus, it's still Sunday. She says text a picture, and then because she's unsure, but thinks we're right to worry, forwards it on to a friend of hers who—though we don't know it yet—happens to be a prominent plastic surgeon we can't afford with an office off the park. Yeah, he says. That's definitely not right. You can't leave it unless you want a major scar.

We've ruined him already. We don't say it, but we're both thinking it. We call the hospital where he was seen to see what they think, and they respond a bit defensively that if we feel we need another opinion that's up to us.

We're lucky, as it turns out. This fancy plastic surgeon also works the night shift once a week in an ER on the Lower East Side. If we come in while he's there, he can fix it. Read: he can fix it under the guise and cost of a simple emergency room visit. We're fortunate. We're lucky.

A few days later, we're in a room with him, us, and a large nurse who looks like a bouncer when the doctor says, okay—this part is going to be rough. My wife and I exchange looks.

The doctor explains, albeit briefly, that the only way to fix what is clearly a problem is to take out the stiches that are already in, that have already begun to heal around the thread. We need to get the wound back open to close it back up right. The next ten minutes are the most excruciating of my son's young life. It takes Sarah, the bouncer, myself, and another passing nurse to hold him down while the doctor works. His cries disturb the whole waiting room, if not the whole street we're on, so loud are they. But when it's done, it is so much better. Years later, his scar is barely perceptible.

The follow-up appointment is at an office with a clientele and furnishings so opulent Sarah says she feels wildly out of place. We're so lucky. Luck and privilege. This is what it takes, I think, to survive life unscathed.

MISINFORMATION: Your uncle's facts about the upcoming election, as with the last, but worse. SEE ALSO: *DISINFORMATION*.

MISSION CREEP: Winging it, military edition. Also, Father Serra, arguably.

MITOCHONDRIAL DNA: Why I, as a male, can prove patrilineal line, but my half sister, whom I recently found on the internet, will have to take my word for it.

MIXED-BLOOD: Always a liminal, despite any number of words they've had for it, no matter how sharp or dull.[100]

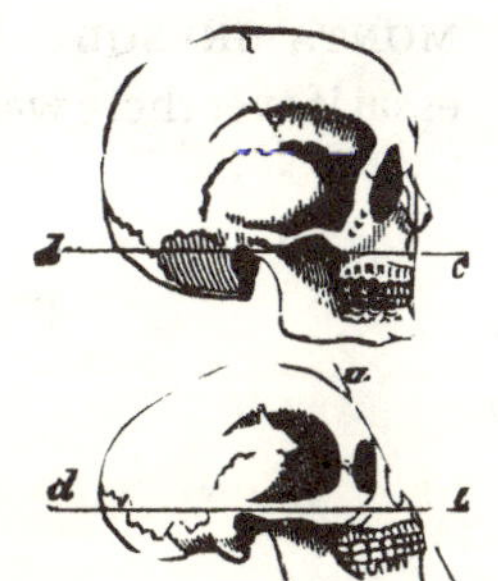

100 We say mutt or we say mixed and we say ethnically ambiguous and you say half-breed and we say Heinz 57 because we have to tie ourselves to a condiment to make a claim about being American and you say coconut or we say hybrid and we say futureface and we say Mestizaje and we say Green Bean because when we make up a term ourselves, we have to repackage a racist trope and Midwest staple to approximate a belonging you say mongrel so much that sometimes we say it too and we say mixed race, or blood, or ethnicity, or we say tell me what part you see in me so I can tell you about the other don't let it be forgotten don't forget me and just don't call me just white we say not that I'm not part white just not only white we say biracial you say miscegenation we say multiracial you say unpure and you say unclean or any long list of names that I'm not going to name here or maybe you just say it's fine for everyone else just not when it comes to my daughter and you say without roots and you say confused and maybe I am, but like, with an asterisk named father, not because it had to be so, not because they are mutually exclusive, you say dirty and you say that our very being is destroying something pure we are destroying purity, we say half we are less than we are not whole half and even our own family says, I don't know what all the fuss is about, in my day there was only blah blah blah (something problematic) but what version are you suggesting I subscribe to? But then, in the midst of my research, I fall into an archive of eighteenth-century terms used by the Catholic Church in Mexico to describe various mixtures of races, the percentages, as dictated by perception, most likely, and so deep is the feeling of needing to belong that I am offended by this list, how dare they, how could they, but where am I? Can I find me here because that's representation, even in fucked-up form, that's the power of just appearing on the page, the need to find oneself on this long list of words. And I *can* find me, of course, but that's not where, because a list ultimately leaves you with nothing—no thing at all. I know my claim. I can claim nothing. Which means I am nothing. If you hear me say that I'm something, remind me that I'm nothing. The world will. It can't help itself. It won't let me forget. But only half. Half something. Half nothing. How dare they, how could they, but where am I?

MONTAIGNESQUE: A dictionary that questions dictionaries? To essai if ever there was.[101]

[101] We move just outside of Philadelphia for an MFA program because that's what a modern writer does. I teach, too, because same. We are so peripatetic by this point that the transition is nearly seamless and obligatory. I plant what I can only call non-roots wherever we go.

I'm still trying to write the story about my father and all of my found siblings that I still can't seem to tell. This is still not that book. I worry that I'm bastardizing that book with this one, a mission creep of sorts, and the irony is not lost on me. This part of writing is not going well, but another is: the part where you just spend enough time with your thoughts and feelings so as to figure out your personal brand of fucked-upness and therefore become, as if by magic, less so. Some say you shouldn't write for therapy but that sounds like some shit that a therapist told them. Or their teacher. I say that you can write for therapy but must remember that your teacher is not your therapist. This is not their weight to carry. Tread lightly.

I find in this time that fatherhood suits me. That my fatherly ethos is as a corrective. (Is this all fathers ever though? Then how come we're not making any progress? Or are we, and this slow slog is just what progress feels like?) We're happy together, our little family, an island out in the world. We decide to start trying to have another.

And I'm starting to regret school, the cost of it anyway, the name-brand education bit. It is true that I went back to school because I wanted to get an MFA. I'm doing what I wanted, which was really only to learn how to write. But the bills are stacking up. In my master's program I begin to learn that teachers are people too, and that they're not always right. But something else was happening with writing. The power of it. The magic of it. I was immersing myself wholly and holy in the world.

MOUTHPIECE: Not for the mouth but as a mouth, speaking the buttered prose of another for predetermined purposes.[102]

---

102 In our small township outside of Camden, New Jersey, across a narrow, tree-lined street from a park with a small stream gurgling within earshot, a scene so idyllic as to be nearly saccharine, we have unknowingly moved into the afterward of a traumatic neighborhood narrative. The house across from us is abandoned, or seems so, but once a month, someone shows up, mows the yard, trims the bushes. Who and why is often a topic of conversation. One day, an Uber driver gives an auspicious introduction as he drops me off: *You don't live there, do you?* No, other side. *Good thing, just google it, you'll see!* he says. April 1995, roughly twenty years prior, a fourteen-hour armed standoff with police, in which three officers were shot. Two died.

Officers had showed up that day to Leslie Nelson's house to investigate claims that Nelson had inappropriately touched her niece and pointed a shotgun at her. The officers noticed weapons, came back later. Six officers returned to serve a weapons warrant. And Nelson, described in newspapers as "a transsexual who worked as a go-go dancer" who was "a loner," started firing at them with an AK-47. The stairway of the house was referred to as the fatal funnel. That term sticks.

But the more I read, the more I think of how lonely Leslie might have felt in this town. The Uber driver, who I end up getting again in later months, so small is this town, says he used to always see him around town in a dress. Sitting on the little stone wall at the end of our street. Did she really? I ask. He or she, whatever you want to call it, he says, didn't have a lot of friends.

The story of the officers matters, too, of course. In a photo from the time, nine officers are hiding behind a bush next to the street sign not forty feet from my house. In the next photo there are sixteen officers. Two of the officers shot were brothers, and one of them died. When I do google it, I see a recent twenty-year memorial of the event, dated just a year before we arrived. Their kids are all grown up now.

And the alienated person matters too, so frequent has this become here. The person made to feel alone. The outcast in her own town because she might have seemed different than the rest of them. This, too, is tragic. I don't know anything about Leslie. I'm concerned by the allegations that brought police to her house in the first place, but I can't unknow the long history of people viewed as "non-normative" being accused of sexual malfeasance, just because they're different. I am also concerned about communities that ostracize people for being different, and what that ostracization might do to someone long term. I'm worried about what feeling that alone can make seem reasonable. For two years, this lore follows us. You live where? Sylvan Street? Did you hear what happened?

MUTUAL-ADMIRATION SOCIETY: Currently looking for members. I'd like you if you joined.

MUTUALLY ASSURED DESTRUCTION: That which keeps us from nuclear war and is also . . .

MUTUAL SELF-INTEREST: The most convincing situation in which to actually trust another person, because I can trust only your want to benefit yourself.[103]

[103] But what if perceived self-interest becomes at odds with what it is objectively so, muddied by either disinformation or willful ignorance?

NEGATIVE PARTISANSHIP: Mr. Contrarian goes to Washington.

NEGGING: Because all we know of love is learned in elementary school.

NET NEUTRALITY: The brave new world is a funnel, is a spigot, is a highway, that can be pinched, throttled, shut off, at a corpora—clears throat—I mean government's whims.

NEUROSIS & TRAUMA: The discourse of the twenty-first century.[104]

NEVER FORGET *(PHRASE)*: Any shorthand is itself already a forgetting, relegating response to a compressed and automated process that requires less feeling than a full discussion, gets pushed to something mentioned in passing and on bumper stickers. Yes, never forget, but what is the quality of our never forgetting? When 9/11 happened, I recall being offended by the phrase never forget, because it seemed to be more political ploy than remembrance.[105]

---

104 Someone has to tell me what to do each day.

NOT AT ALL SLIGHTLY SOMEWHAT A LOT

105 But maybe I've been too hasty or maybe it was just too soon. Maybe, especially as time moves on, the compression is necessary because it is impossible for us to feel the full weight of trauma while going about daily life. A way to acknowledge the full container of grief without letting it spill each time. I feel this, it says, perhaps, but more fully later.

NO-DENIAL DENIAL: A dance of sorts. A game at play. But decidedly not accepting responsibility.[106]

[106] Here or around here a new president is elected. I'm taking a class with a professor who happens to be Jewish. Already her fear is palpable: what this could mean. I, too, am worried. I, too, have concerns, but not like her. It is as if she sees the full scope of it already, how bad it will get. She says so, too, that night. Even years later, it is amazing to me how much foresight she had at this very moment, a premonition for exactly how bad this will get. For much of these years, I'll have to resist the urge to ask her, but what's next? What happens next? It is not her weight. She has her own.

For my second semester I try to teach a composition class themed on the "Post-Truth" era. Within a week it is clear that I'm in over my head. I just hadn't really realized how deep misinformation had already traveled, how entrenched the positions, how shallow the source. Students most clearly read any news as reflections of their parents' views and news habits, of course; still, I wasn't prepared. My intention was not to point students toward one side or the other, despite obvious alliances here, because I don't think that is how you change minds. Still, in not presenting which side is clearly spreading misinformation, all I've taught is false equivalence.

NO-FLY LIST: One of many algorithmic rule sets that can determine modern life, including: secondary screening list, the selectee list, the terrorist watch list. From a list of sixteen people originally deemed "no transport" a movement is made. Also, my internet search history must be an algorithmic nightmare from researching this book. (Searches: how does one know if one is on the no-fly list?).[107]

[107] In a teacher-training course that we were required to take, somebody asks how you could help a person who has written a paper that is, for example, I don't know—racist. A group of largely white middle-class kids are all outraged. One kid in the class says they'd help them. Everyone starts to gang up on him. But I agree with him. I say as much in class and everyone ignores me to keep going after him. But what I mean is, I say, I don't think there is any room in academia for racism—or anywhere, actually—but I also don't think you change people's minds by telling them they're wrong. We can arm them with information, we can help them down a path, but ultimately, the change has to come from them. I believe that when you try to make a racist account work it fails every time. That rational thought and science can prevail.

But I have failed to account for bad faith. I have failed to account for bad research. I have failed to account for how alluring it is to simply point to someone else as the cause of your problems, how seductive that can be for people. And increasingly, the glut of information making it harder to distinguish the good from the bad, a legitimate source from an illegitimate one. And with this president, everything is different. Because the cognitive dissonance that it takes to believe any portion of what he says is greater than I could have ever anticipated.

NOMINATIVE DETERMINISM: That your job was predetermined by your name. **SEE ALSO:** ***NAMING INCONGRUENCE.***[108]

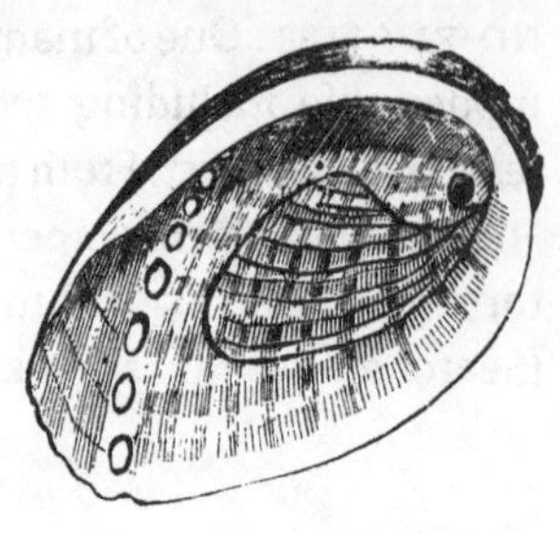

108 My name is water. I am a water sign, if you believe. I don't. But I cannot deny that when I drowned as an infant—my breathing had stopped, but my heart had not yet, I'm told, liminality even then it seems—it was in a tub with my brother, my mother down the hall on a telephone call, though she says it was not like her to leave us. I can still hear the heavy whoosh of the water. I don't see neglect here, and you shouldn't either. (But what is me feeling the need to say that really about? Why do I rush to preemptive defense?) I see the plight of the single, teenage mother, holy thou art. I will forget this aquatic trauma, this underwater grave, the time spent in the hospital, for years. Won't even come up. Buried deep, submerged, presumably, in the subterranean structure, until as a teen, in the ocean, caught in an undertow, a flat wall of a break, as they do at 15th Street, a California beach I'd come to hundreds of times before, enough to be local, enough to know the wave's embrace, and how you must succumb to them, let them take you, or swim sideways, but never, no matter what, panic—but this one, this time, so much worse, and I don't know how one believes or doesn't believe in magic, or the great repressed, or the undertow of the soul, all I know is that getting out of the water, this time, when I did finally make it out, with the help of a passerby who heard my screams for help, something in me released, inexplicably, and I was afraid. Suddenly and fully afraid, not just of this wave, this time, this proximity to something lost, but of some previous experience. I knew, somewhere deep, what had just nearly happened, because I'd experienced it before, and knew, wholly, holy, that this was deeply close. I don't know what to make of a water name and a water sign and a water fear that is more awareness and respect than even trepidation and maybe only one of those things is real anyway—I only know that I feel, if not a kinship, an understanding that from water I came and from water I shall one day, most likely, return.

NON-APOLOGY APOLOGY: I'm sorry you feel that way.[109]

NON-FUNGIBLE TOKENS: (1) For sale: a book with one copy. (2) One of the low-level anxieties of this time is that some people are making astronomical amounts of money out of new technologies that seem as if they are manifesting from thin air, while others are still struggling for even a living wage, doing age-old work. (3) That from a utilitarian perspective, humans are absolutely fungible to the broader system—necessarily so, even—but on an individual level, we swear by our non-fungibility.

---

[109] I know many writers who don't or didn't need an MFA, people who are so talented or well read or versed in craft that they know much of what can be taught in these places. This was not me. I needed to be there. I needed to drown myself in these conversations. And I needed to read. Beyond how I'd read before. I'd spent no real time with work that didn't call or cater to me explicitly. I'd spent no time being challenged or grown by work, and none pulling apart texts for their inner machinations. I needed to learn of the histories of literature, the conversations, the trends both before and during my lifetime. And I needed to learn to be comfortable with what I didn't know. That not knowing is a wonderful operating position for any author. To become less sure of my opinions while simultaneously becoming *more* sure of my own craft. My scholarly journey was, in the end, an education in unknowing.

NOTIFICATIONS: Whether user, context, or system generated, whether push, passive, smart, or otherwise, you are likely approaching inundation. Would you like to be notified when you've become inundated? Would you like to set a reminder to learn more about notification management?[110]

NTH DEGREE: Once you've decided to take it there, it's to any required power.[111]

NUDGE THEORY: One person's nudge is another's manipulation, which is another's encouragement, itself another's paternalism. Do nudges diminish autonomy or encourage monotony? But choice architecture can be constructed such that we have already limited available options by which choices we have to begin with. We must become nudge literate. Nudge detectors. Nudges are created to lead to specific outcomes which is fine unless you had different outcomes in mind. Plan accordingly. SEE ALSO: *ALGORITHMIC NUDGING*.

---

110 SARAH: Alexa, cancel notifications.
ALEXA: Okay, cancelling notifications.
SON: Alexa, what are notifications?
ALEXA: (Asks for clarification.)
SON: (Marches off, unsatisfied.)

111 Sarah starts to feel the burden of the clock. We discuss another child and she tells me that she believes it to be now or never. We try and nothing happens. We find a doctor who wants to do tests, and then wants us to try harder. He's casually misogynistic, practically gives me an award for my sperm count in the first two seconds of our meeting. Far from comforting, his congratulatory tone just makes me think of my father scattering his seed across several states and all of the siblings I've found so far. I'm still processing this as he physically turns to Sarah with a *Now let's talk about you* face. He tells her she hasn't conceived because she's a Type A personality. He tells her that it's because of her job, she's too stressed. Sarah leaves knowing that it's all her fault, because that's essentially what the doctor said. But "Don't stress," that doesn't help. This will be the last time we see him, unhelpful as he was. It takes weeks to recover from how he made her feel. We move before we can get any further anyway.

OBJECTIFICATION: You are an object.

OCCAM'S RAZOR: The simplest solution first.[112]

OCCUPY: A movement.

OFF THE GRID: Life *on* the grid can be so tiresome, overwhelming, *un*-lifelike, that for some the most humane solution is to opt out entirely.

[112] We've only been here a year when it's already necessary to decide what's next, given the school year and the application cycle. We're here, and we're not here. We are still in New York; we are still in Kuwait; we are unforgivably Californian, but we're trying to be present even as we have a foot out the door for what's next.

I decide to pursue a PhD because I still can't write the story of why I'll never have children, even as we plan for our second. This is hilarious. This is also the strange magic of writing, I think: that I can explore and expand myself in the physical world by spending significant time sitting in and articulating the specific traumatic weight of a previous iteration of myself. I am growing in the process. I am grown by the process. I am processing, I suppose.

But it's not just that. When I first started back in school the idea was that even if I didn't sell books—however unlikely that seemed—I'd be able to teach. And in these years, both of these plans dissolved as careers and turned into the adjunct hustle. And so I'm also doing a PhD because I have now fallen into the trap of student debt and it's the only way to stave it off. I certainly can't pay it off working as an adjunct lecturer.

OPTICS: But how will this look to people? A decision-making process we'd discourage from an average ten-year-old, now serving as the guiding principle of a modern society.[113]

ORTHOSOMNIA: When your sleep suffers because your sleep tracker criticizes the quality of your sleep getting.

OTHER: That there is an inside and an outside in which all are positioned.

OUT OF REACH (PHRASE): Once, that a person might not be within immediate proximity of a phone. Now, the anxiety felt when a phone is not within immediate proximity of a person.

OUTSIDE THE BOX: To think differently. Note, there is no inside the box. Nor is there a box.[114]

---

113 We move to Texas, for yet another school. It is a fascinating commentary on America that our rent hasn't changed: a one-bedroom apartment in New York City (and subsidized by the school at that) = a two-bedroom house with a small yard in South Jersey = a four-bedroom house with a large yard in Lubbock.

Lubbock turns out to be remarkably similar to Kuwait City. Truly. They should be sister cities. That's how that works, right? Someone just comes in and says, you know what this reminds me of? Anyway: sandstorms, the brutal heat, religious intolerance. Maybe intolerance is too strong, perhaps just insistence. Something like: we are a godly town at our core and as long as you respect that we won't have to be ungodly. Even local laws prohibiting the sale of alcohol were only just repealed a few years prior to our arrival. Four hours from anywhere and flat land as far as the eye can see. Oil industry booming not too far away, and oil money driving home values up. Organizing your day around avoiding the sun. Televangelists on TV as ubiquitous as the call to prayer from the mosque.

114 In our new home on the outskirts of town, where the dust blows in such high volume from the cotton fields that the lawns actually raise by inches over time, it takes a year and a half to settle in enough that we're searching for doctors again. Conversations begin again about how to solve what are now referred to as our fertility problems.

OVARIAN RESERVES (AS IN DWINDLING): A phrase the doctor uses for one of the reasons having children gets harder with age.[115]

OVERKILL: Too much killing.[116]

OVERTON WINDOW: Not what should I say, but what are the range of things I can get away with having said.

OXFORD COMMA, *THE*: A hill to die on.

---

115 There is a canyon-sized gulf built into this semantic structure, as if he is whispering it from across the street to lessen the blow. This is not a female who is increasingly producing fewer eggs due to advancing age; it is a part-time platoon in a bunker, whose help is called on to serve in dire circumstances; or maybe it's gold hidden in a hill somewhere that we use to set an index. But the point is, it's extra. Doesn't it imply extra? These reserves are extra. Surplus. So, you see, you aren't without, you just simply don't have the extra spare excess that you previously had, and it's not as if they're gone anyway. They're simply dwindling, like in a fairy tale. Like traffic. Like savings. Like population. Like the potential size of a familial unit. It's not extra at all, is it? The doctor says there are eggs here, but not many, and fewer tomorrow.

116 We think we have great health insurance, but maybe we simply haven't had cause to call or push on it too often. But for a couple of years, we have that confidence of a safety net. Because our health insurance covers infertility, we discuss it. If it gets there. We began an IUI regiment, which means a lot of shots and a lot of waiting. We're told that the shots basically run an assist on getting the sperm to the uterus, but little more. It is a cost-effective start. It is, our doctor suggests, the start of making the case for IVF to the insurance company. Apparently, we need to make a case. And because I've taught rhetoric the phrase *Everything's an argument* is never completely out of mind. We must hurry, the doctor suggests, but be sure to relax because stress, too, is a procreation inhibitor. Hurry and relax. But hurry. You're killing your chances. Hurry. Relax.

P

PANDEMIC: It's catchy. And then it crosses a threshold.[117]

[117] On December 31, 2019, in Wuhan, Hubei, China, doctors report a cluster of viral pneumonia. In a small Texas town, we celebrate the New Year by banging pots and pans outside. It is a tradition that my family has always done, but side-eyed Sarah finds it, I fear, a bit low-rent. She only slightly objects, as if worried about the neighbors hearing. Because of my son's age, his midnight happens at 9 p.m. I can feel that it's the last time I'll be able to convince him of this. It is already a day after Dr. Li Wenliang warned his colleagues that the viral cluster presented like SARS.

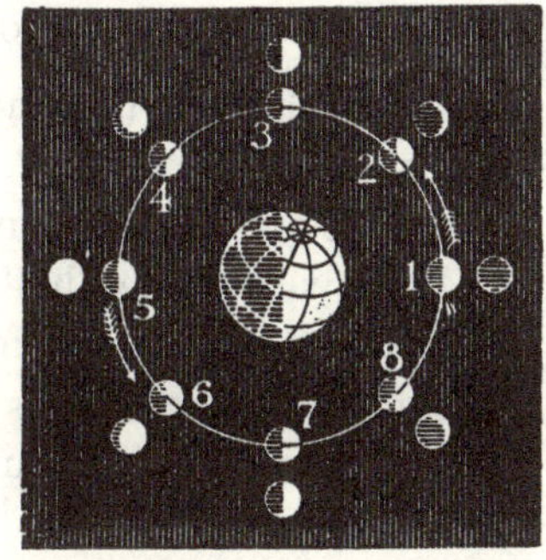

PANOPTICON: Because thinking you're being watched is more effective than knowing that you are.

PAPERCUTS, DEATH BY A THOUSAND (PHRASE): Studies have shown that the amount of time it takes to read user agreements we encounter in every day life is so great that almost no person would likely be able to in earnest. Unless, of course, you can work them like a full-time job for at least a month a year. The notion of the user agreement, then, is facetious because it is impossible—not just improbable—to read them.

PARADIGM SHIFT: Said to be the case more often than it ever could be, primarily as a function of the sayer's excitement level toward that which is being said.[118]

PARENT CORPORATION: But how do you know when you're ready to be one? Is there ever a right time?

[118] On January 11, a sixty-one-year old man in China is reportedly the first person to die from complications of the coronavirus and the world hears it like white noise. Students are arriving for a new semester. I'm tweaking syllabi. I'm answering emails. It is already a day after Dr. Li Wenliang has begun to show symptoms of the virus himself. He is hospitalized on January 12. On January 21, the first reported case in the United States is reported in Washington State. By January 23, Wuhan, a city of 11 million people, will be cordoned off entirely. By January 30, the World Health Organization declares a Global Health Emergency.

PARRONDO'S PARADOX: You've got to lose to win.[119]

PASSING: Whether via name or by skin tone, another paradox entirely. And deep. Inner. Conflict. That one doesn't appear to be what one is or vice versa. And I'm guilty of this, too, dear reader. At a lunch with my new half sister, I assume that her mother must be black, so different are our skin and hair, though she assures me that this is not the case. It is just the fluctuation in our genes. And I think I offended her by saying it. Foot in mouth, forever.[120]

---

119 One of my sisters has been trying to have a baby unsuccessfully too; for a year or so, we actively don't talk about it. They recently tried IVF, got far enough along that they named the eggs, shared pictures. In the end, it didn't take. It's hard to talk about.

When she hears we've been having similar struggles, but also that our insurance will cover it, she responds with disbelief. She wants to know what insurance we have, she wants an explanation of benefits. It's frustrating for her because they have only budgeted to try once. She doesn't say it, of course, not all of the words. It's in the questions she asks, the tone of the response. We compare prices of IVF off insurance. She is in L.A. and the cost is roughly $30,000; in Lubbock it's about $12,000. I tell her come live with us for a while. This stuff is heartbreaking, particularly for women, who often carry the additional burden of feelings of guilt. I'm comforted by our insurance, that we're taken care of.

A week later, we receive word that our health insurance company is refusing to pay for IVF. Our doctor thinks we should appeal the decision, says that ours is likely one of the strongest cases he's seen for it. The first step is for the doctor to file an appeal stating our case, which he says should clearly be approved. He does so.

120 How could I ever explain the low-key anxiety of performing racial identity in a real-time response to people's perception? The closest I can come is Reception Theory, but for people instead of books. We who dance the race meridian.

PASSIVE INCOME: The new American Dream.

PAY-IT-FORWARD: A theory of altruism that has the unfortunate, cynicism-inducing distinction of having also been a feature film (and yes, a book before that). As an enactment: rather than repay an act of kindness one has showed you, a person would instead pass that kindness on to someone else in the manner they see fit. SEE ALSO: ***HELPER'S HIGH***, ***GIVER'S GLOW***, and phrases so shiny that you wish you hadn't started this thread at all.[121]

PAYWALL: Because there is way too much for free on the internet. The castle wall, digitized. Can you afford the news and can you afford not to.[122]

PEARL-CLUTCHING: The action you do while saying you would never.

PETER PRINCIPLE: That everyone, given time, will be terrible at their job. Plan accordingly.

PETTIFOGGING: Not a make-out session in inclement weather, sadly, but a lawyer, lost in the details on purpose.

PING: A digital breadcrumb.

PINKWASHING: A certain Southern chicken chain at a Pride Parade.

---

[121] A study across 130 countries found that "people who spend a bigger proportion of their money helping others are generally happier, in the long run, than those who spend it on themselves." Doesn't that "in the long run" qualifier just stick out like a sore thumb though?

[122] When several leading newspapers begin to make their pandemic coverage free, it is meant to be a gift. Look at our altruism. But also it's a tacit acknowledgment that when information is important enough, it should be free to all. Perhaps they should lower the digital rampart—pay*wall* proving to indeed be the perfect word—and start a Kickstarter instead? The people are at the gates.

PLAUSIBLE DENIABILITY: Trying just enough to say it's not so.

POLITICALLY CORRECT: Politically incorrect to say so.

POLITICAL THEATER: All the war is a stage.[123]

POLYPHARMACY: Using multiple drugs to treat one ailment.

PORTMANTEAU: Mash-up whose requisite parts are no longer necessary.

POST-ETHNIC: Would that it were.

POST-HUMAN: Your body, afterward, but possibly in a new *during*.

POST-LAPSARIAN: Everything after.

POSTMORTEM: Originally, an inquiry as to why a body is no longer animate; now, the meeting after the meeting to discuss the meeting (regardless of the animated status of the bodies involved).

POST-TRAUMATIC STRESS DISORDER (PTSD): These times, all of us.

POST-TRUTH: If we can just skip to the post-post-truth part, that would be great, though perhaps I haven't thought fully enough of what that could mean.

123 Hygiene Theater, too, will soon be a political prop, though at this precise moment in our narrative, its need is only just arising.

POWER-GRAB: Sadly, not the most offensive grab suggested by a president.

POWERNAP: All the time you need, so long as it's quick and doesn't take long.

POWERS THAT BE: A vague offering up, a surrendering to an unseen force.

PREDATORY LENDING: Or, as bankers call it, lending.

PREDATORY LISTENING: Or, as governments call it . . . [124]

PREDATORY PRICING: Or, as salesmen call it . . . SEE ALSO: *PRICE-GOUGING.*

PREEXISTING CONDITIONS: All of your ailments before the current one.[125]

PRICE-GOUGING: Taking a $13.50 pill used to treat a terminal disease and raising the cost to $750 per pill. Hypothetically.

---

124 When someone mentions to me that Alexa's settings are such that she hears a significantly larger amount of daily conversation than one might think, I begin to test her. First thing in the morning when the house is dark and I'm up by myself I take to walking into rooms or down halls and whispering so softly as to barely enunciate at times, *Alexa, can you hear me?* Mostly, she does.

125 I am less concerned about my problems than I should be.

NOT AT ALL SLIGHTLY SOMEWHAT A LOT

PROBIOTICS: The belly brigade, the family flora, an attempt to harness gut bacteria, a large market with as of yet unquantifiable benefits.

PROPORTIONAL RESPONSE: A justification or mental positioning whereby an attacker might allow themselves to feel morally right as they decide to kill people, simply by comparing one killing to another.[126]

---

[126] On February 4, it is my birthday, and the Chinese Supreme People's Court admonishes police for punishing a group of eight doctors accused of spreading falsehoods about the virus, including Dr. Wenliang, who will die in three days. Someone's social credit score suffers, presumably. It's a Tuesday, so I teach and hold office hours and tell nobody of my celebration because I am still sensitive about being older than my peers. When I mention this project, which is not supposed to involve the virus, one of my officemates—who is from China, whose name is ████ but who goes by Gabbie to go easy on Texans—says that the word the Wuhan mayor used to describe the outbreak in a recent news story was a word with connotations of accepting—but also decidedly not accepting—responsibility for the outbreak. She can't recall exactly what the word was. It vanished to her shortly thereafter. My ears perk up. This business is slippery, I think. We look for it, together, the word, on tiny dueling computer screens on opposite sides of a small, windowless room. But the word is gone.

My professor lacks clarity about an assignment; a student tells me I've done the same. On NPR, they mention the first recorded death from the virus outside of China, but it sounds small and distant. I sit in my car on the second floor of a parking garage watching 1,000 or so students navigate between classes. I fixate on the word *recorded*, and that the recording sounds small and distant. Like vinyl. Like an eight-track. Like a wax cylinder. Like a phonautograph.

PSYCHIC NUMBING: On a scale we can't feel. The way we dismiss death/harm/hunger as it moves from one to two people, and how much greater with each additional body. Less human, more abstraction.[127]

[127] If there's an early internet origin story of our inhumanity toward each other it's this: people fighting and trampling each other for TVs at Christmas time. To google "Black Friday fights" is to request a visceral punch in the stomach. Yes, this appears to be the worst part of humanity. People pitted against each other to save money on a product that they do not need in any strict survival sense. But Black Friday is an encroachment of business in the first place. They could manage this, the stores, if they cared to do so. We understand crowd control. We know how to make a line work. They must choose not to for fear that to lose the frenzy could lead to a loss in sales. The videos are uploaded, and we click. Not all of us. Not anymore, maybe, though we still shop at these stores.

PSYCHOLOGY OF POVERTY: If one's past relationship to cash truly affected economic behaviors determining one's relation to future poverty, I could've never gone and invested in all these lotto tickets/credit cards/Beanie Babies/Iraqi Dinar as a retirement plan. I'm good—promise; just don't start nudging me about it.[128]

---

[128] We're warned that it's a bad idea to proceed with the appeal process while also moving forward with the treatments, that the insurance company—even if you win, which is unlikely—makes it hard to recoup the money after the fact. People don't like to give money after the fact, whatever the fact. We wait one cycle, which is a month, to see if anything changes. Bureaucracy is slow, so it doesn't. We decide to move forward with the doctor while simultaneously trying to fight the denial of the claim. The doctor says he will get the paperwork together.

Years back I had a friend who used all his student loan money to buy guitars, amps, and studio equipment. He had a dream to start a record label that made no money, like as a policy. He was in luck, some dreams being more achievable than others. His friends all gave him a hard time about buying all of his equipment on loan. King of the Big Purchase, we called him.

When we decide to pay for IVF with my student loan money, it's not even a hard decision. We don't have the money in the bank, except for this money I'd held onto. It is not a smart financial move, but maybe you'd be surprised how little that matters when you're fighting against a clock. It's a lot of money. Still, once you've decided to have a child you're already committed to spending for nearly two decades. In America, that's $12, 980 per year, according to current FDA statistics. $233,610 over eighteen years, before inflation. It can be quantified, more or less. Once you've grappled with this, the IVF decision feels more akin to an upgrade, adding on the cushy floor mats, or expedited delivery, perhaps. We begin by doubling the amount of Sarah's nightly shot regimen.

PUBLIC RELATIONS: Not *re*, but *manipu*. You are a Target market. You are being targeted.[129]

PYRAMID SCHEME: Not selling product to the people, but selling the person who will be selling the product to the people.
SEE ALSO: *GETTING IN ON THE GROUND FLOOR*.

[129] United Airlines flight 591 from Orlando to Los Angeles makes an emergency landing in New Orleans when a passenger onboard has a heart attack. Except that it's not a heart attack, passengers deduce, after overhearing the wife of the man say that he had lost his sense of taste and smell and had been feeling ill before the flight. A man gives CPR midflight. The flight continues on because the man had affirmed in a pre-flight questionnaire that he had neither tested positive for COVID, which was true, nor felt sick, which was, apparently, not. Many other passengers get symptoms, though the CDC never reaches out. The man who gave CPR has symptoms and nobody reaches out. Two days later United announces a new policy to work in conjunction with the CDC on getting more information from passengers to increase contact tracing. In the press release they say that this new initiative represents the airline industry's most comprehensive collection program to date. They call it "industry leading," and they mean it. The program is entirely optional. Passengers must opt in.

QI: The only word I can consistently play on *Words with Friends*, an app-based game you are supposed to play with strangers, but I currently only play with myself. A life force, both in the game and out.[131]

QUACK: Someone not worth listening to or taking seriously.

QUAGMIRE: A precarious position, land that moves underfoot, and an anachronistic cartoon neighbor.

QUALIFIER: A type of hedging, possibly.

130 The inclusion of this letter should not be read as any sort of a nod to, about, or around any recently hatched conspiracies. It is not a wink. It is not even an acknowledgment of this non-mention, rather, it is an abecedarian obligation and nothing more. It is an acknowledgment of that which falls between P and R.

131 I have friends.

NOT AT ALL	SLIGHTLY	SOMEWHAT	A LOT

QUANTIFIER: Is it large, small, partial, inclusive, negative, indefinite, comparative, partitive? Is it cardinal or ordinal?[132]

QUARANTINI: The new isolation cocktail.[133]

QUICK-AND-DIRTY: To guarantee the latter by prioritizing the former.

---

132 Siri, Alexa, Cortana. Is it that we all instinctively know a great need to be mothered, or is it simply the bias of the makers reiterated?

In a recent *Guardian* article, Ivana Bartoletti, founder of the Women Leading in AI network, says, "An algorithm is an opinion expressed in code . . . if it's mostly men developing the algorithm, then of course the results will be biased." In light of the overall number of women in tech and reports of wide-scale misogyny in the sector, it's safe to assume this is not a great start. So, there are problems on the design end, but that's not all. In the same article a USC sociology professor suggests that these AI "personalities" are "a powerful socialization tool that teaches about the role of women, girls and people who are gendered female to respond on demand."

This is what I'm left with: who is this woman who has moved in with me and what is she teaching my son?

133 It would take another dictionary entirely to address all of the quarantine-specific lingo that emerges in these months, largely portmanteaus or riffs off more common phrases. The covidiot, the pandejo, quarantine and chill. COVIDbabies. Elbow bump. Several linguists are cited in a BBC article noting the ways we use language as a coping mechanism in times of stress. (Is that how this project happened?) We're witnessing this in quickened time due to global reach. There's a German phrase, one linguist notes, to describe the never-ending policy debates that have taken over during these times: *Öffnungsdiskussionsorgien*, meaning "orgies of discussion."

QUIXOTIC: (1) That a Don Quixote dictionary exists. (2) That this word is not in it.[134]

---

[134] We get up at 6 a.m. to head to the hospital. Our son goes next door to the neighbor's house to play with their four kids. In the car, there is a palpable fear sitting between us of what we will do if there are no eggs. This isn't logical given the doctors' assurances, but it's the constant worry that Sarah's body will betray her. She has the seat-heater on, because it's still cold out, and I joke about the possibility of poaching them. An absence of eggs is illogical in light of all the injections I've been administering nightly, but it permeates every step of the process. What if the body just doesn't do it?—whatever *it* is at the current stage—she wonders aloud. Often. A problem too when stress can be an inhibiting factor to the process. So, we joke, or I joke, to help, careful to straddle the line of seriousness. It's Valentine's Day, and aside from the cold sterility of the process, both of us encouraged to give our samples by people trained to treat you with cold, scientific distance, precisely because they are so physically close to you, it can be romantic if you frame it so.

There are now cases in twenty-nine countries, if the twenty-ninth country is a cruise ship in Japanese territorial waters. The CDC says there are 600 more people in quarantine and a new confirmed case at Lackland Air Force Base, and we still have a houseful of stuff somewhere out in the world that is waiting to come to us. I wonder if there was any toilet paper or masks in there because we could be mid-COVID-19 rich and not know it. Paper goods rich. Not likely, I think. The freeways were empty. It was dark when we arrived; either the hospital hasn't fully opened, or they're conserving energy. We seemed to be the first guests in this morning. Or visitors. The virus is out there, we are just starting to learn, but not out here. Not yet.

After the procedure, when we exit, the news is on in the now-crowded waiting room, and they're discussing something out there with the volume down. It's getting louder. Not the voices, but the faces. They're beginning to contort. Bigger, angrier, louder, even when muted. The chyrons increase panic because how many banners can a screen even hold? They nearly create a Droste effect with their picture-in-picture semantics. The TVs are increasingly on wherever you go, but no *real* fears yet, just ratcheting tension. There is something out there, but not here. In five days, a president will suggest it will be warm by April and that'll pretty much wrap this up. So, chill out. Calm down. Relax. Nothing is out there, and nothing is coming.

QUOTIDIAN: Wake. Eat. Sleep. Repeat. TV. Sleep. Eat. Repeat. Wake. Repeat. Some potential exposure. Repeat.[135]

[135] A 2015 report states that people have grown more individualistic and that as a result, they test 40 percent less empathetic than people in the 1970s, hardly a bastion of empathetic times itself.

R

RADIO SILENCE: Is sometimes just good policy.

RAP SHEET: Should you have one: a haunting, a stalker, an inescapable weight that follows you everywhere you go; should you not, a noir trope so common as to induce laughter.[136]

[136] The new rap sheet is no rap sheet at all. Four times have I seen this recently: a [redacted] finds himself on the original list of [redacted] [redacted]; an assistant professor at [redacted] [redacted] accusing a [redacted] [redacted] and the school's lawyers will only protect the involved professors and students in certain circumstances—not even the [redacted] will name him; I hear a rumor that a guy [redacted] is accused of [redacted] but not until [redacted] [redacted] learn that his [redacted] [redacted] [redacted]; on the aforementioned [redacted] [redacted] So much silence. [redacted] A lawyer says: If you see something, don't say something.

RATIONALIZATION: A manufacturer at full output or an excuse we tell ourselves, including, but not limited to, why a manufacturer might not be at full output.[137]

REALITY: In TV, a representation of nonreality, sculpted to appear as heightened reality, which, when folded into actual reality, becomes self-fulfilling prophecy. Also, now available in virtual, augmented, or mixed/extended realities, non-, semi-, or fully immersive.

REAL TIME: The time that passes at the speed in which you're reading about its passing.[138]

RECEIPTS: The proof is in the purchase of the pudding.

---

137 If at some point in the future you see me out in public with my son, and you happen to overhear him say something about a Dry Danny, just know that rather early in the pandemic, after months of near-total isolation, it became necessary to create a non-lubricated version of the Wet Willie. Please play along.

138 Getting together with friends is important to me.

NOT AT ALL SLIGHTLY SOMEWHAT A LOT

REDLINING: Not the lighthearted nickname for joyriding the original trolley cars of Los Angeles, but the systematic denial of services to minority groups in Los Angeles and elsewhere. When someone says, "Get over it; it happened a long time ago," simply show them a map of how it perpetuates.

REDUCTIVE: A defining characteristic of late capitalism. Bottom-line it for me. Let's get down to brass tacks. Land the plane. Give it to me straight. Get to the point. Get down to business. Get to the nitty-gritty. Tell it to me like I'm twelve. What's your end goal, endgame, endpoint? Cards on the table, no beating 'round the bush, talk turkey, where's the meat of it? What's the number? Get to the number and get there fast.

REDUNDANCY: Either built-in preparation for potential problems or a person who can no longer do their job at maximum output. Also, built-in redundancies are perhaps the single most defining characteristic of late capitalism.[139]

[139] Inuits have more than 50 words for snow, or 500, depending on who you heard it from; this is the myth that's true if you look with a squinted eye or add an asterisk or unfurl the caveats, caused as much by there being a variety of Inuit languages as it is by the varied types of snow. It depends how we define *word*, too, apparently. David Wilton's *Word Myths* dedicates four pages to this one myth alone. He says that it feels true because we know that there are some things that we have multiple words for, and it confirms bias because it originates by talking about someone we don't know. Us and them. According to Wilton, this myth is true, even if the details of the myth are often exaggerated or confused. It is true but not for the reasons people thought.

REGRETS, *NO*: Originally as much a joke as a tagline to sell T-shirts, now a mantra of entrenched position, seemingly stemming from the belief that the cumulative effect of even bad decision-making has yielded the present version of self, and to have a regret, therefore, is to wish to negate some portion of the self, insecurely.[140]

---

140 February will come to be referred to as the lost month for a president, the month when inaction, misrepresentation, and lack of a clear plan sets the United States down a particularly fraught course. It's not so much that we were caught flat-footed as that he denied we even had feet, fired all the sock-makers, then acted like the world was divided about the benefits of shoes.

While global cases of the virus jump from 12,000 to 85,000, he tries to solve it with rhetoric that points fingers. He tweets 900 times in February, presumably with the best thumbs, mentioning the virus in only 20. Each mention either praises his own response or criticizes those he sees as opponents for theirs.

February is lost to us, too, for different reasons. Mainly, we wait.

We are assured that we have eleven eggs, a high amount. They take my sample and introduce the sperm, and we wait to see which achieve blastocyst stage. We wait for a call each day from a kind doctor who gives us the news: eleven eggs become ten viable candidates and one lazy one. Then eight, plus a quitter, and a couple of try-hards. Within days, seven grow to a satisfactory rate, still ahead of the 50 percent attrition rate the doctors suggested we prepare ourselves for.

We pay $2,500 for a PGS—currently rebranding as the PGT-A test, good luck getting that to stick—a test that does little more than count chromosomes. There should be twenty-three pairs, or forty-six total. You're looking for euploid, not aneuploid, which would indicate a whole missing or extra chromosome, which is where serious health problems can begin.

When all is finished, there is one healthy fertilized egg left.

REGULATORY CAPTURE: A fox in the henhouse charged with the task of keeping foxes out of the henhouse.

REPETITION: Is also a type of magic. We can be soothed by, we can create muscle memory, we can numb our minds, we can lose ourselves wildly in the rhythm of pattern.

REPRODUCTIVE AUTONOMY: Historically denied as a means of controlling sex. SEE ALSO: *SEXUAL AUTONOMY*.

RESOURCE: Assets, generally, but increasingly, a reference to a person only as an asset.[141]

RESTRICTIONS APPLY: King of all caveats, found as much in the fine print of the Constitution as it is on a Happy Meal.[142]

REVERSE MORTGAGE: An equity eater and monetary sleight of hand normally pitched at the elderly by a TV personality they vaguely recognize from their youth, which suggests that they can afford to live only if they agree to lose everything at death. *You can't take it with you anyway* is a fine enough sentiment, but this also willfully ignores the way that it can halt generational progress within a family.

RHINOPLASTY: Long-term nose esthetics.

RHINOVIRUS: Short-term nose esthetics.[143]

---

141 *Human resources*, itself an alienating phrase, the part of the company supposedly set up in defense of said resources, but often is a slippery bugger working to manage said resources toward maximum exploitation for the benefit of the company. This is not in the brochure.

142 In the Preamble alone: *we, union, justice, tranquility, common defense, general welfare, ourselves, and our posterity*. Not a single word there about freedom to do what you want to do just because you want to do it. Rather, freedom by virtue of our mutual obligations to each other.

143 I call my mom and discuss rising concern with her. "It's just the flu. People are so stupid." She's not wrong, I say, in an attempt to appease her, though I believe that she is. I decide to push it a little more than I normally would with her, as this time it seems important. We get in a fight when I suggest she is not the spitting image of health as a retort to her being unconcerned. We don't talk about it ever again, not directly.

RIGAMAROLE: So many words that they begin to obscure meaning.[144]

---

[144] In March of each year, the AWP conference draws the nation's top writers and writing programs to a major U.S. city. Because it's in Texas this year, our school, department, and literary journal have a large contingent set to go. Months back, I booked what appeared to be accurately described as a mansion: pillars, pool, palm trees. Vacation logic: look how cheap it is when divided by sixteen people? Yes, it is true that this huge house was cheaper than sixteen hotel rooms, though it is fair to say that I would not have otherwise had cause to put sixteen hotel rooms on my credit card. It sounded like the best idea at the time, and now it could be a recipe for disaster.

This year the conference is at the San Antonio Convention Center, thirteen miles from Lackland Air Force Base, where the government has been quarantining potential COVID-19 patients, primarily from cruise ships. The CDC has an extensive plan to mitigate risk to the local population by quarantining these travelers for two weeks and making them test negative twice before leaving.

In the week before the conference starts, a woman is released from quarantine after two negative tests and goes almost directly to the North Star Mall. She chills at the food court, she zigzags on the ol' escalators, she walks among the throng of the hoi polloi, and why wouldn't she—she has been cleared. We are not a police state, although we play one on TV. Her third test comes back positive, and panic begins.

The flood of texts and calls about our trip is not insignificant: everybody begins reaching out to everyone else with every update that they have heard, read, or lifted from the wind. My phone is blowing up from fifteen different sets of concerns, and all I can really think about is that I can't afford not to go on this trip because I'm sure the Airbnb fine print is not likely to let me get a refund. It seems fair that each person would only be out their money if Airbnb won't refund it, but I am also aware this will only hold if people are reasonable and don't try to stick it all on me. I reach out to the owner of the house, and she seems generally disinclined to consider such things.

AWP cares that a bunch of writers should not be the epicenter of a breakout in San Antonio that goes national, perhaps, but mainly it seems that the optics would be bad. The conference cleaves in two, and the suggestion is immediately made online that those who are still planning to go to the conference don't care about those with compromised immune systems.

In the following hours, rumors fly. First everyone is told that the conference will be scrapped altogether, then others will suggest that was never true, and broadcast that the event is still on. There are rumors of a meeting with the mayor, and infights between various positions within the larger organization about what the right thing to do is. For hours, we follow these threads, and each added text or phone call results in people changing and unchanging plans, a fluctuation I feel in my wallet, but only potentially.

I reach out to the owner of the house again to check in on local conditions. *It's fine out here, hon. Everything's completely normal. See you soon. Hon* and *Sir* are two deeply Texas cordialities that I distrust on instinct. "See you soon" feels like a reminder that I'm obligated.

I go, and everything is normal, though the owner and I never see each other. I wonder if she's holed up somewhere outside the city. I go and see family on the south side of town, three miles from Lackland. I stop in to meet my grandmother for the second time ever. She doesn't remember me and truthfully, we shouldn't be allowed to visit old folks' homes if we're going to big conferences by day, say, but I don't know my aunt well enough to tell her *no* to anything. But this is what it's like in the weeks when it's both happening all around us and not yet happening at all. We go, and it appears everyone is fine, but it is tough to prove a negative. We go, and our hands crack and bleed from so much sanitizer. We go, and it's the last time anything feels normal.

RINKY-DINK: An etymological search starts lighthearted and gets bleak fast: mickey-moused, jury- or jerry-rigged, a whole slew of critiques on ethno-engineering, which becomes a list of people complaining that they can't casually use ethno slurs anymore. This is our internet.[145]

---

145 Could an AI learn to be ethno-phobic? I mean, it's not a problem if it's a stationary computer, perhaps; it is when it's *ANYmal*, the seventy-pound doglike AI that has trained itself to run faster. If bias exists in the coders, why couldn't it be inserted into the code from which an AI learns, even if inadvertently?

When my grandfather got old he got racist, either slowly or just at increasing volume. Or maybe he just gave up on having a filter. I'd never known him to be racist previously, but this is what it began to feel like. All of his brown-skinned grandchildren stopped wanting to be around him; some stopped seeing him entirely and I couldn't help but assume that this might have been why. When we moved him back from Arizona to California after he could no longer take care of himself, his daughters and I would drive him to appointments at the VA. He liked to lament the number of Mexicans who had arrived since his departure from the state a few decades before—to his brown-skinned grandchildren. He did this loudly, so as to make a point, in waiting rooms, leaving me, his half-breed grandson, to apologize for him in broken Spanish and English. That's how I picture him, small and feeling justified enough to not feel great about his grandchildren and making them apologize for him to people they more closely resembled than him. This was not the cruelest thing he'd done in his life. It certainly painted how we felt about him at the end. Why, for example, I was the only one of his grandkids who would take him to appointments. The others wouldn't put up with that shit. But that news network of the family Canus sure sings a sweet siren song, if you happen to notice the world is changing around you and maybe you're not the center of it anymore. Dog whistle is appropriate.

He never said it, but I always wondered if it was because all three of his daughters had terrible relationships with men who happened to be brown. If maybe the seed was planted then, but he couldn't say it. So he waited, maybe, until there was a news channel that could justify his small feelings inside. *See, other people see it too. It's not just me.*

Is it sitting dormant in the code already? Is it possible?

ROAD RAGE: A particular anger caused from extended time in traffic, despite driving having once been thought pleasurable. Predominantly young and overwhelmingly male. Anger brought on by the many stressors of traffic. How do you cope with stress? SEE ALSO: *AIR RAGE; BIKE RAGE; ROID RAGE;* or *RAGE RAGE.*[146]

ROLE-PLAY: It may be worth it to just act nice occasionally, even if you suspect you're actually not.[147]

RUBBER-CHICKEN CIRCUIT: A politician chasing down dollars.

---

146 The Arroyo Seco Parkway was the first freeway in the United States, though if you blink, you'll miss it. It now exists as a sub-section of the 110 Freeway, which travels from Pasadena to downtown L.A. to the Port of Los Angeles near San Pedro. It conjures another time. On-ramps start from stop signs. The road is twisting and narrow. If you squint, you can still imagine what it must have been like to drive this windy road, with no other car in sight, on a leisurely Sunday ride in the 1940s.

In 1987, a deadly year on L.A. freeways, the term *highway hostility* is born. It dies shortly thereafter, presumably of too many syllables. The term *road rage* is coined the following year, but remains stagnant, its hard alliteration an engine idling. The phrase is used in popular media only 3 times before 1994, when it is used on 27 occasions. An engine revs: 500 uses in 1995, 1,800 in 1996, 4,000 in 1997. But are the incidents of violence increasing, or is it that language and its propensity to travel have caused the term to move so rapidly?

According to AAA, the numbers are rising, at least partially the result of an increasing lack of sleep. We just need naps.

147 At AWP I meet with a publisher about a translation project I'm working on. She appears to be a white woman, but I know to be suspicious of this assumption. I don't lean into my Spanish pronunciation, though I know it. She corrects me. It's fine, I think, that this white woman is correcting me on something I already know, something that is supposed to be more culturally mine than hers. (Even typing that feels problematic but is truthfully something akin to what I'm feeling.) But it doesn't feel fine. This tendency to not lean into Spanish pronunciation when I'm speaking English stems from youth, when to do so was an affectation. It gets under my skin when people do it. It is, at its heart, meant to be a move toward authenticity. But now I have a new problem. Now that I've studied Spanish for several years, it's actually less authentic for me to not pronounce it correctly. This is going to take some time to digest. Either way, she is not wrong in her correction, though it feels wrong to me. A negation. At the heart of this is being uncomfortable making a claim for what is essentially half of my personhood.

S

SABBATH: When the day of rest becomes instead a day for grieving for all the work yet to come and all the rests untaken.

SAFE SPACE: A space in which people can feel confident they'll avoid persecution for perceived differences but whose very existence highlights that the rest of the world is not so.[148]

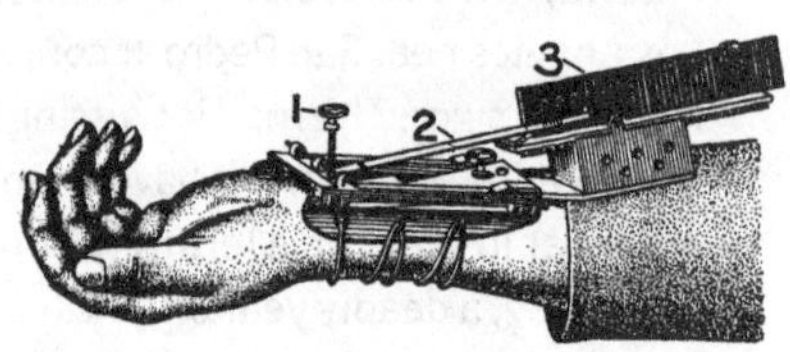

[148] The head of the English department decides we should all meet in the second-biggest classroom in our building to discuss how we will no longer be meeting in large groups. A hundred or so show up, and his opening line is how we probably shouldn't be meeting like this. We shouldn't. I still find it comforting. The school has decided to move all classes online—35,425 or so students is no small change. We are given a task—to take care of our students, to comfort them, go easy on them, emotionally but not academically. Winkyface.

They extend spring break by a week, and prices fall out of the airline market. Some students decide an extended Mexican vacation sounds great and will get stuck there. A group of more than 200 students from the University of Texas go to Cabo San Lucas, and one in four contracts the virus. The company the students had booked through, JusCollege, sent messages to the students beforehand citing how safe they were, that there would be no change to their refund policy, so . . .

In my own neighborhood, people don't take it seriously. My next-door neighbors have guests over often. People come to the door to discuss what's going on in a way that would be sweet if it weren't so troubling that they are possibly bringing a deadly virus straight to us.

On March 17, the mayor confirms two local cases, one in Lubbock County and one in Hockley County, both travel related. That will become important. Community spread—that's the one you want to watch out for in these early weeks. I learn it on the now-nightly press conference. When the numbers grow big enough to be disheartening, they'll stop holding the nightly live televised press conference and move it to midday and online.

Still, it's prudent to begin a shutdown. The information trickles in; it seems certain that the government is trying to mitigate panicking by slowly ratcheting up how serious this is. No groups of 1,000. Then the next day 100. 50. By the end of a week, they suggest no groups of 10 or more. It happens that fast.

In America, for a few brief weeks, the nation feels nearly unified in our obligation.

SALESMAN: Of the variants snake oil, blue sky.

SALTY: As with the sea, even if I were to attempt to desalinate myself, I fear the chemical byproduct and cost-prohibitive nature of the process would render it unsustainable long term. I am, alas, a salty individual.

SCAREMONGERING: Spreading stories to frighten, but later, an accusation by which to question the motives of someone sharing information—perhaps necessary and scary—that one simply might not want shared. SEE ALSO: *CAREMONGERING*.

SELFIE: A self-image we use as illusion, or an illusion we use as an image of self.[149]

SELF-PROMOTER: Shameless. But let me tell you about this project I'm working on . . .

---

[149] When something good happens, I get excited.

NOT AT ALL SLIGHTLY SOMEWHAT A LOT

SELF-SABOTAGE: Any of many things we do that get in the way of any of many things that we want to do, often at the behest of a little voice we wrestle inside ourselves that tells us why we can't to begin with.[150]

SEXT: The most private text message you'll ever send with the potential to become the most public, determined entirely by the arbitrary whims of the receiver.

SEX TOURIST: Not tourism, but opportunism. One who does in their neighbor's house—and to their neighbor—what they wouldn't dare at home.

SEXUAL AUTONOMY: Historically denied under the guise of controlling reproduction. SEE ALSO: *REPRODUCTIVE AUTONOMY*.

---

150 Only in America could a person return to school, get three degrees culminating in a PhD, lose so much financially and socially, and render themselves nearly unemployable. I didn't do it for work anyway. I did it for me. I did it to see if I could. I did it to use as a blowtorch on that chip on my shoulder that I know—believe me I know—I'm supposed to have outgrown long ago. I did it to grow, and maybe write a book. Maybe to tell my story. This still isn't that story, though it's part of it now. I do know that I am not the same person anymore, that school has, in fact, changed me.

We have a Zoom game night because COVID, and my best friend doesn't hesitate to tell me that I have indeed changed, but when he says it, it's an accusation. Old B wasn't like that. Old B wouldn't feel that way. We were talking about the vaccine and if we'd get it when we could, and I mentioned that of course I would and that it's our responsibility to. You've changed, man, he says. Never has something that I've wanted to hear so bad felt so terrible when I did.

SHADOW BANKING: Non-bank banking intermediaries, credit derivatives, synthetic credit derivatives, sub-sub-sub-prime. Also, banking in the drive-thru around 4 p.m. or so, when the sunlight directly in your eyes inhibits view of the screen.

SHARED MEANING: Agreed-upon messaging. SEE ALSO: *SAME PAGE*.

SHARENTING: Not the division of time by parents across two Christmases, but rather the modern practice of a parent putting too much information about their children online, sometimes to disastrous effects. Aka *over-sharenting*. SEE ALSO: *TMI*.[151]

---

[151] On March 16, a president begins an aggressive campaign to rebrand COVID-19 the Chinese Virus. You can feel how bad he wants it. A person in the press corps snaps a photo of his notes for the day, and a childish hand has crossed out *corona* and handwritten *Chinese*. The FBI says they believe there will be an increase in hate crimes against Asian Americans: "The FBI makes this assessment based on the assumption that a portion of the US public will associate Covid-19 with China and Asian American populations."

March 16 is also the day we go in for the egg implantation. They have already begun limiting elective procedures, our nurse says. They're meeting about it again today. It takes a second for me to register that this means us, elective, that we're getting in under a wire. She says our doctor has stopped services for all patients but the women furthest along in the process. Lucky you!

In the end, it is the second to last day that this hospital will even perform any elective procedure in an attempt to lessen strain on the medical facilities and by March 22, the governor will suspend them throughout the state.

SHOCK AND AWE: Mainly shocked by how awful it is.

SHOCK DOCTRINE: Using times of extreme turmoil to push through policies that you could not otherwise. SEE ALSO: *DISASTER CAPITALISM*.[152]

SHOOTER KITS, ACTIVE: The new American backpack.

SINGULARITY: Where space-time gets fuzzy, but the fuzziness nevertheless remains important. Also, the hypothetical moment when the robots ~~took~~ take over, oops.

---

152 NOW SHOWING!

SITUATIONAL ETHICS: If I seem inconsistent it's just because I'm trying to figure out the positioning that best benefits me. Carry on.[153]

SLIPPAGE: I did not mean to reveal that about myself.

SLOWBILIZATION: Signs that perhaps the new global economy is not inevitable after all.

---

153 In recent years, the contingent of anti-vaxxers has grown, largely due to misinformation spread online. Pseudo-science. It's ironic that it is people being vaccinated that has allowed for the illusion that vaccines aren't necessary. There is no vaccine for this yet, but it's coming. We hope it's coming. We do hope for this, right? Even though they're rushing it? I mean, I'm not trying to be first in line or anything, but we will get it. But for the anti-vaxxers, what hope do they have that this can go away? How do they see this ending, I wonder?

WE CANNOT LET THE CURE BE WORSE THAN THE PROBLEM ITSELF. He yells it at us, just like that. He appears to be messing up a Francis Bacon quote. It sticks anyway. My neighbor says it to me when she's bragging about what stock she intends to buy with her stimulus check. We're thinking oil while it's down, she jokes. I tell her I think the idea is that we blow it all on curly fries and blue jeans, but then go ahead and pay off my credit card anyway.

And in these weeks, the COVID vocabulary again expands: we must flatten the curve; we need herd immunity; we have or do not have cabin fever as we shelter in place. Does COVID-19 refer to the iteration or the date established? I thought it was COVID-2, I thought it was coronavirus, I thought it was novel. Wait. COVID-19 is the disease, and SARS-CoV-2 is the virus, but when we call it, we just call it corona.

The World Health Organization website says that from a "risk communications perspective," they're worried that calling it anything approaching SARS would have unintended consequences, because people might remember the last one. So they've framed it as "the virus responsible for COVID-19" or "the COVID-19 virus" to help you.

Whew, I thought the conflation of terms was just my confusion, not like, say, a strategy.

Soon we are in the midst of an explosion of disinformation, misinformation, anti-information. In a series of daily televised press briefings, it is so clear that a president is lying, solely to protect himself. The superlative prez strikes again: the best words, the nicest masks, the smartest people, all while citizens are starting to die. The clearest failures, the nicest obstructions, the biggest mistakes.

SMALL TALK: Conversation that purposefully avoids being meaningful. Part of . . .[154]

SMOKE AND MIRRORS: Deceit, involving neither smoke nor mirrors.

[154] We need to take a pregnancy test to see if the process has taken, but it's done by blood draw. I can no longer accompany Sarah on procedures due to strict rules at the hospital, where they also have a COVID-19 test center. It is really only measuring HCG levels. On the morning of March 26, before we take the test, we talk about anything but the test so as not to jinx the test. We've also been holed up together long enough that we've said nearly all that we have to say to each other. Nothing new is happening but the daily news and the weather, so we do that version: small talk.

The U.S. surgeon general says that an increasing supply of necessary medical equipment won't fix this. "We will not supply our way out of this problem," he says, like we're twelve and gluing masks to trees because we don't get it. He suggests that we already have capacity, but it's just misaligned, which is so bureaucratically neutral that one wonders if anyone will ever take responsibility. They won't. He does indicate that the way to get out of the crisis is to lower demand, which seems to suggest that some of us should just lean into it and die. Is that what he's saying? We don't have death; we have life, just misaligned.

The test comes back positive.

On March 30, we have nearly 3,000 deaths in the United States, and to present a strong front, a president hosts CEOs in the Rose Garden. Reporters liken it to an infomercial, though it doesn't appear anywhere near as professional as all that. It's closer to sketch comedy.

They all shake hands and stand in close proximity, just like a vice president won't wear a mask when visiting staff at the Mayo Clinic a few weeks later, just like a president won't wear a mask when touring a mask-manufacturing plant shortly thereafter. The message clear: these rules, these deaths, they're for the people. They will not get us.

SNACK: When a person appears so desirable that you want to consume them; however, notably, reducing said consumption to that which one might ingest on the go, in between more substantial meals, a meta-commentary on desire itself.

SNOWCLONE: Any number of phrases that can be readily adapted for other use. Includes, among others: the gates, the stans, and "X is the new Y" phrasal constructions.

SNOWFLAKE: A thing of such singular beauty that it must be repurposed as an accusation.

SOCIAL CONTRACT, *THE*: Our success depends on each other, a basic premise behind why you can't simply do whatever you want, whenever you want to, and other things we tell children that adults increasingly seem to struggle with. One solution is to create a . . .

SOCIAL CREDIT SYSTEM: Your reputation, ranked. A value system based on an extension of nudge theory with origins in policing. You are given a grade on everything from paying bills on time to how you treat your neighbor, and if you are not careful you won't be able to take the express train again until you raise your score. If you are rated untrustworthy, a travel ban may be placed on you altogether. SEE ALSO: *NUDGE THEORY*.[155]

SOCIAL DISTANCING: All this time I thought I was depressed, it turns out, I'd been in training.[156]

SORRY NOT SORRY (*PHRASE*): Worse than simply not sorry, a stubborn recalcitrance often tinged with *schadenfreude* that the other is bothered to begin with. AKA *FAUXPOLOGY*.[157]

---

155 In a move first announced and piloted in 2014, China planned to have all citizens ranked by 2020. One wonders how a person's COVID-19 status might affect their ranking. How does speaking out about it rank? Finally, what curve might a government grade on? Thank you in advance for it not being money.

156 This is a joke I tell my students in our last class before all classes are cancelled. It's funny, to me. It works well in the first class and falls flat in the second, a problem that often happens, I find, when I try to treat two separate roomfuls of individual bodies as if they are the same.

157 Our insurance company denies the appeal the same day it is received, and we wonder if they even read it.

SPACE-AGE HAPPY BIRTHDAY SONG: Congratulations / on your rotation / around the sun / another time /May your orbit / stay important / to your distant satellites (sung to the tune of "You are My Sunshine").[158]

SPECULATIVE FICTION: Sci-fi in a bow tie. Outer space, but practically.

SPIN: A polish you put on something to make it appear what it isn't. Also, all claims that positions are "no spin" should be read as peak spin.[159]

SPITE HOUSE: Any house can be a spite house if you try hard enough.

STARE DECESIS: The legal process of deferring to case precedent because for some, "doing what you've always done will get you what you've always gotten" is not a scary sentiment.

SUICIDAL TENDENCIES: Are your loved ones okay? Are you?

SUNDAY SCARIES: The feeling at the precise moment when Sunday-Funday remembers Manic Monday.

SUPERPOSITION: That the order in which things are buried is the order in which they happened. Arguably, not a super position for my therapist.

---

[158] The CDC recommends you sing "Happy Birthday" to yourself while washing your hands as part of their official instructions on how to do so correctly. I recommend the space-age version; it's a little longer.

[159] I have an accurate understanding of my problems.

NOT AT ALL　　SLIGHTLY　　SOMEWHAT　　A LOT

SURGICAL STRIKE: A military attack distinction that matters more to the sender than the receiver. Also, potentially, when not enough anesthesia is used.[160]

SURNAMES: For some, a solid foundation on which to build, a legacy to tie into; for others, grains in a sandstorm, shifting as needed. The matronymic and the patronymic, reflections of cultures, stories, and legacies that we tell, hide, or are sometimes cursed to repeat.

SURPRISE MEDICAL BILLING: Worst. Surprise. Ever. Bills that can't get worked out between hospital and insurance provider, left on your doorstep.

---

160 After the pregnancy test, we have to wait to do an ultrasound to determine if there is a heartbeat. This is the next step toward making sure that the process is still viable. We're worried though.

A few days earlier, Sarah interrupted me, mid-class, on Zoom. She'd cracked the door open just enough for me to see her eyes and mouth, eyes frazzled, lips pursed. I think I just lost the baby, she says, trying not to cry before pulling the door shut again.

It was potentially just out of view of the computer, but I couldn't be sure. I looked off-screen, then back to the class. Twice. What must my face have shown? I quickly turned off my camera and walked out to find her hunched over in the bathroom crying. She's bleeding heavily. She can't figure out what's happening. And there's clotting, which makes her question, too, what she's even seeing. She knows it's bad, she says, and I have to convince her that we actually don't know anything without dismissing her feelings, though I, too, am worried about the blood.

The first ultrasound is done the day of my son's sixth birthday, a day we otherwise spend in quarantine. I have to stay home with him because no one else can come over. Sarah drives herself there and gets the test done under what the hospital is calling *heightened conditions*.

My son's friends do one of those parades they show on the internet where the parents drive by slowly and wave balloons and signs out the car window. It's sweet. It's also a problem because they all want to hand things off to us and we're really trying our best not to bring things from outside inside the house. Our kindness becomes a safety risk as we take what they offer.

For three days we wait. We don't discuss. There seems to be nothing I can say, or, maybe it's best that I just say nothing. Tread lightly.

SURVIVOR'S GUILT: Right at this very moment.[161]

SWATTING: The prank call has not changed in 150 years; its consequences have.

SYMPATHIZER: An accusation. Originally from war. What business do you have feeling anything for the other side?

161 Part of the guilt here is that we're bored. We're put out. It is unfair to say. It is unkind. There are people who have died, are about to die, are dying. We are hidden indoors. We are fortunate to be somewhere where we can do this. We are having groceries delivered and we are wiping down the bags with disinfectant. We are incredibly privileged in this moment, geographically privileged, as it turns out; it didn't seem so when we moved here. Meaning we aren't making any more money than we have in the past few years, but thankfully we aren't living in NYC when this happens. Which means we have bedrooms. Plural. Which means we have no neighbor banging on the ceiling anymore because a child is playing. It means, even though we are in deep red country where the neighbors on both sides aren't taking it seriously and keep coming to the door to see if our son can come out and play, we do have the privilege of a backyard and we can go out there for much-needed vitamin D and I can place a ladder by the fence so they can yell their play at each other when necessary. And we do: over-the-fence flower delivery, over-the-fence water balloons, over-the-fence snowball fight. It's awkward but it's safe.

And still no results from the ultrasound.

T

TAKE IT TO THE NEXT LEVEL *(PHRASE)*: (1) That there is always something further to strive for. (2) Heaven, for example. (3) What would you be doing at this level if you didn't think there were more beyond?[162]

---

162 I'm trying to finish the last classes I will take as a PhD student, the last in this return to school. I'm trying to finalize my reading list for my qualifying exam, which I hope to take in the fall, which means I need to read 100 books over the summer. I'm trying to time this according to when a baby will be due. I'm trying to write translations. I'm trying to tie the *Aeneid* to the fact that my father's parents were migrant farm workers from south Texas and he was born one picking season, out of state. I'm trying to translate the work of a poet from Uruguay because of her ties to Mexico City in 1968. And because they called her Madwoman. Mad like Mahboulla. Mad like crazy, though maybe mad like angry too, so vocal was she as a proponent for students' rights and unions. I'm trying to finish a teaching pedagogy class. I'm trying to get a position as an assistant director because I think I can help with the fall semester and I hope I'm interviewing well. I'm trying to be a good father to my son. I'm trying to be a good husband to my wife. I'm trying to help her in her pregnancy that we are blessed to have. I'm trying to not get Zoom fatigue. I'm trying to not get the virus. I'm not saying it's overwhelming, I'm saying it's hard so far already and no end in sight.

Sarah feels like she's going to vomit the entire wait for the ultrasound results. I feel like someone who needs to soothe someone into not feeling how they feel, which feels both impossible and selfish to consider at all. If the third day is hard, the fifth is insufferable. Then a sixth and still no answer. She finds it hard to eat, which she knows is problematic too. We wait.

TELEPHONE GAME, *THE*: A game that illustrates how the words we say to each other evolve with each telling, normally veering away from accuracy the further down the line they go.[163]

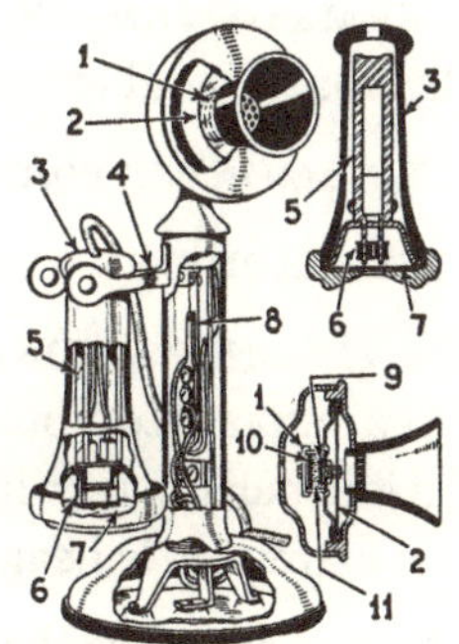

TELEVISION DINNER: The first sign of the future was non-food served on a non-plate cooked via non-flame, after which we barely needed to rely on each other at all.

TENURE TRACK: A job and a unicorn.

163 Early on we are told it's a good idea to mask up. Then, rather quickly, when there is a run on supply, we are told not to wear a mask. That it isn't helpful. Unnecessary. People yell at each other on the internet as to why this should be obvious. This among reports that people are hoarding so many masks that now hospitals and doctors can't obtain any. A few weeks later, they say we should wear masks, and people yell at each other on the internet as to why this, too, should be obvious. It's about the asymptomatic spread, but conspiracy theorists see this as one more point where either the government or the media—depending on which side you are cleaved too—is currently manipulating the situation. And the pounding of the Gish gallop grows louder on approach.

TERMS OF VENERY: A collective noun for animals, primarily used by hunters and writers.[164]

TESTIMONY: A conversion narrative.

TESTIMONY, SWORN: A narrative with the power to convert.

TEXT GENERATION: That your favorite journalist will soon be an AI program. Computer-composed works. Still in its early forms in journalism, it so far works best with data-heavy articles, like reporting Little League baseball scores.

TFW: You realize that writing books, too, is a sales job.

THEATER, HYGIENE: Fake it till you make it.

THEATER OF THE ABSURD: The human desire to watch war on TV, for example.[165]

THEATER OF WAR: You break it, you buy it. Metaphorical viewing that becomes literal in the Iraq War, televised war in real-time. Get your popcorn.

---

164 A murder of crows, a shrewdness of apes, a plague of grackles—a frown of humans. That's all I can come up with for us. Maybe a scowl.

165 A president recommends taking hydroxychloroquine, a malaria drug, to ward off the virus, says "There's a rumor out there" that it helps. "If it were me, I might take it" he says, but when it is, he doesn't. On April 24, a president suggests injecting disinfectant as a way to combat a virus. He wants to know if the sun can help us. He wants to blast it with light. Later, when people make fun of him for it, he'll say he was being sarcastic. He's not alone: claiming sarcasm, hyperbole, joking are all covers people give him when what he is saying is obviously false and inflammatory. This is where he grows.

THERAPEUTIC INDEX: Difference between the effective dose and the deadly dose.[166]

THERE ARE NO WORDS TO EXPRESS *(PHRASE)*: Indicator for the failure of trying to.[167]

---

166 At least one person loses his life after ingesting too much chloroquine. A president won't be cornered into saying whether he is actually taking it himself, but he suggests he is, which is quite convincing, if you believe him. He's not just the president, he's also a client. Snake oil. "What do you have to lose? Take it," he says. You must train yourself to hear his qualifiers. If it were me . . . I might . . . rumors are . . . a lot of people think . . .

When the first scare happened, our doctor immediately doubled Sarah's dose of all hormones. It didn't help her already fragile state. Plus, the pain of twice the regimen of daily shots that I administered nightly. Once they confirmed heartbeat, they switched doctors from the fertility specialist to an OB-GYN who could monitor and deliver. Her first appointment is just genetic counseling, which we've already had. The takeaway, she says, is what she's already heard: you're old, prepare yourself that this may or may not work. At her first appointment with the new doctor, stressed, hungry, hormonal, they couldn't find the heartbeat. Sarah reads, with great stress, the signs of the doctor getting worried too. For ten excruciating minutes. She says it felt like longer. As it turns out, the baby was hiding. Somewhere at the bottom. "Whew, I was getting worried," the doctor said. "She's gonna give us a run for our money." Sarah left the appointment shaky, all of her feelings of something being wrong and the blood and the clots and how sick she was feeling; like walking a tightrope; on pins and needles; edge of her seat; do or die. None of these seem to suffice.

167 Or maybe sometimes there are no words to express. Or perhaps we're all so rushed that we know the words are out there but don't think another person will be patient enough to watch us find them. That we don't have time to write them as well as we might.

When the test results come back, it's fine. And we are five weeks' pregnant. No, she is, to be sure, but I am five weeks' something else. I'm not sure if there is a name for it.

But she's fine, they say. The doctors give a list of reasons why the blood could have happened. It needs to be monitored, but we're okay. Don't stress. Stress makes it worse. The statement stresses us out. The blood was likely just X, or Y, or Z. We are not out of the woods. We are in the woods. Still, it's good news. Stop stressing. Are you eating okay? You need to feed the baby. The baby is a grain of rice.

THING(S): Possessions.[168]

---

[168] The word *thing* is a non-specific term for a tangible, inanimate occupation of physical space. Space, too, likely feels non-specific, but it's not. There are natural things and unnatural things, but mainly when we say unnatural what we mean is artificial, unnatural having different connotations. Supernatural things are another can of worms entirely—which is, itself, a collection of natural things in an artificial thing, unless the can is made of, say, hemp.

Most of the time, artificial things belong to people, and natural things belong to no one, or *god*, who is the archetype of a supernatural thing, of course. After you own a thing, you get something else—then you have two things. This will repeat in greater or lesser degrees until the day you die, at which point you will have *no* things, or rather those things will suddenly be had by someone else. Early in your time, you'll spend it collecting things. Then later you'll start offering to give all the things back in exchange for more time. Time doesn't work like that; it's concerned with neither you nor your things.

It becomes important, for logistical reasons, that you collect all of your things in one place. After a while, you move all of your things to another place. This will happen from time to time. This change is indicated by a new alphanumerical construct. Everyone who used to seek your presence via one geo-locatable index will suddenly use a different one, or they'll use the old but find someone else at that location. Lately, this data will push to varied data-interpreting tools, though it was, for most of human history, an analog process.

If you're not careful, you will start to share things, including the alphanumeric geo-locatable construct itself. If this happens, you will also share the things inside, maybe because you bought them together or were gifted them as a pair—in which case you technically own half a thing, but now's no time to be petty—and sometimes another person just sort of stands by your things long enough that you can't remember whose was what as of when.

You may even create a new mini living thing as a byproduct of all that thing-sharing, and though that new thing will begin by appropriating your things, it will eventually procure its own things and spaces in a cyclical process mirroring your own. All of this can start to make you feel like half a thing too, half a person, half an identity. That's a good thing to some and a bad thing to others. You should really write your name on things, though, just in case.

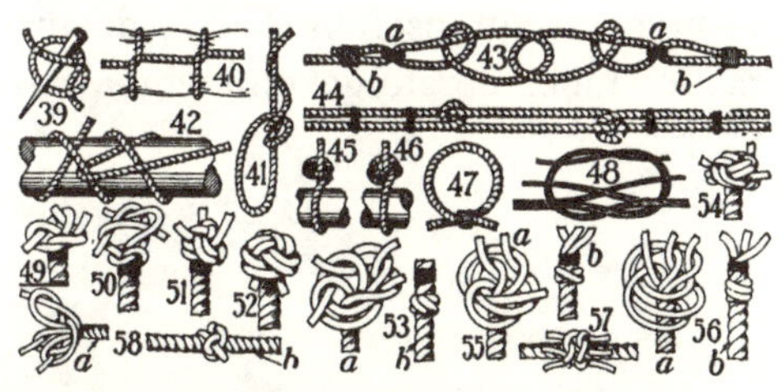

THOUGHTS AND PRAYERS: As a canned response, insufficient. Yet, I have no better alternative to offer. I've tried *well wishes*, but it sounds too glib. *Hopes and dreams* has a nice balance, but sounds too cheesy, also doesn't really work contextually, implies one's hopes for their own life as opposed to what others might wish for you. I've tried *thinking of you*, but it feels too romantic. *Keeping you in our hearts* might work, but does sound old-timey. The point here is thoughts, yes, but not prayers. That doesn't sound nice, though: thoughts, not prayers. As if to say I am devoting headspace to you, but not to your god. My first problem is that anyone who knows me knows that my *not praying* is not a passive act, but a conscious decision, a move away from the church. I know such phrases are not about the sayer, but the biggest problem with reaching out to someone at all in these hard times is that if your attempts sound disingenuous, you could make it worse. In this way, any mention of a thing that is not like you to say (e.g., praying) can strike the exact false chord that one is hoping not to convey in this moment anyway.

THOUGHTS, NOT PRAYERS: See? What kind of a monster would write this? *Sorry for your loss. Sending thoughts, not prayers.* The only way I know how to resolve this is to revert to the original saying.

THROTTLE: Purposefully slowing down one's access to information for corporate, governmental, or other bureaucratic purposes.[169]

---

[169] What does a full breath feel like, I wonder, for most people? I would be obsessive about checking myself for symptoms if I didn't realize on the very first day that I have nearly all of them all the time anyway.

Except for smell. I can still smell things. But as to breath, it is the denial of oxygen to the brain, to be honest, that most concerns me. That is likely the cause, I'm told, of all of these headaches. There are solutions. A rescue med or inhaler inhaled quickly, but I can never get the timing right. What I am saying to you is that breath is always, always labored. When I'm not overweight. When my lungs fill with air, it is a half-fill, if anything, that not even the mask I now need to sleep can truthfully fix, and most days I wonder, simply, if I'm doing it right. I research how to convert a CPAP to a ventilator because it's a good time to have a plan.

When lungs fill with song, it resonates, a heavy and deep timbre to its sustained notes, though I cannot oblige any longer than necessary, and maybe not that much. It is the voice of a deep hall in a basement somewhere.

When my lungs fill with anger, or the hot intent of it, anyway, fiery and charged, it is a short-lived wheezing. It is a short game we are playing, so hang in there.

When my lungs fill with fluid, as happens with nearly every caught cold, you can hear its burrowing. It grows thick and is hard to listen to. Rattle. Stridor, the doctors say. The kind of cough that makes someone joke *You dying*? And you say *living* but think *maybe* and cough a crowded, overly syllabic laugh into being, a jazzy off-time percussion to it. We don't talk about it, really, but Mom says matter-of-factly, *Well you've just always been that way. Couldn't take you to a public pool without you catching everything in it.* So get on with getting 'cause that's just how you are. Because of the jaundiced birth? Because of the asthma? I ask. Because of always living in places with mold so deep you could see it on the walls, because of the drowning so young? Maybe it's that water, still in there.

Whenever I am sick or broken, if I sprain a finger in a way that allows for complications from a tired lung, it is this thing that keeps coming to me. When my lungs fill, this. This is on a clear day. This is in a perfect world. This with and without a normal flu. This.

THROUGHPUT: In manufacturing and computing, rate of production leveraged toward efficiency and maximum yield. SEE ALSO: *RATIONALIZATION*.

TIRED: Perhaps the single most defining characteristic of late capitalism.[170]

TMI: As an observation, now, arguably. As a notion, that revealing personal details is frowned upon or can result in negative consequences.

TOO BIG TO FAIL (*PHRASE*): Arbitrary socialism for business, not for people.[171]

TOO SOON (*PHRASE*): Anything at any time for someone. Plan accordingly.

TOUGH LOVE: When love is about to not feel like love.

TOXIC MASCULINITY: That there is one way to be a man and it is built of broken parts.

---

[170] Getting things done during the day is important to me.

NOT AT ALL SLIGHTLY SOMEWHAT A LOT

[171] Let's see. So, corporations are people, and that which is not yet a fetus are people, but illegal immigrants are not people, nor are those in the Axis of Evil who are of course just collateral damage. Incarcerated people—largely of color in otherwise rural, white voting districts—are temporarily not people come Election Day, but are definitely people during the census, making them ghost constituents. Ghosts, of course, were people but become phantasms. In the search for a consistent through line in your rationale I see only . . .

TOXIC POSITIVITY: (1) Positivity that isn't helpful or presumes to know more than you without qualification. (2) Positivity that suggests that you aren't looking at things correctly, haven't framed them with the right perspective.[172]

[172] I can only ask her when he's not around. She has no inside voice or sense of discretion. So I approach in the late-night hours, or when he's in the backyard playing on the Slip 'N Slide, as he is now. Not sneaking, just cautious. I watch him through the window, the water splashing around him, and ask softly.

Alexa, how many people have died today from COVID-19?

This might answer your question: according to Reuters, as of today, May 7, 2020, there are 3,794,907 cases of novel coronavirus worldwide. Additionally, there have been 263,669 deaths and 1,195,828 recoveries. The countries most affected by this outbreak are the United States, with 1,237,347 cases, 73,792 deaths, and 195,541 recoveries; Spain, with 239,301 cases, 26,070 deaths, and 128,511 recoveries; and Italy, with 214,457 cases, 29,684 deaths, and 93,245 recoveries.

It takes her over a minute to answer completely. Then she's silent.

I know what I asked, and that she didn't answer, but I don't push. And what I want to remember most is that though we are taking it seriously, and though it's day 52 in lockdown and frankly, we're all a little bored, it is an incredibly privileged position to feel so. And that most of the messaging I'm hearing is about people who are not taking it seriously. I don't want to forget that. That solidarity is peeling off in waves. That now, even people who are framing sheltering in place to flatten the curve as reasonable are saying, *Yes, but here is my personal experience, and maybe it's not so bad. We need to open the country, because Freedom.* And that is where the feeling of being alone comes from. Not from being isolated physically, but emotionally. This may be the biggest thing we'll ever face, until the next one, and if we can't get together on this, then what is the point?

TRANSFER, EMBRYOTIC: The medical process of putting a fertilized egg into a woman in hopes of pregnancy, not to be confused with transference, which is putting your feelings about one person onto another, commonly a therapist.[173]

TRIGGERED: People triggered by the term *triggered*—and blind to the irony of it—is the moment we are in.[174]

---

173 By the third day of June, we are out of the first trimester, the riskiest time. The baby is slightly larger than a lemon. We crossed the threshold of 100,000 deaths in the United States about a week ago, if you believe the data, which multiple states are reporting poorly. Slide. It appears that they are conflating numbers to improve the appearance of testing. They are omitting testing areas that are known to have high counts, like homes for the elderly. Slide. A news crew is arrested on live TV and it surprises no one that is the channel a president doesn't like. How quickly we are sliding...

An election is coming, and the obfuscation is happening in broad daylight; a president uses executive privilege to control the social media he has exploited for lies, when they suggest they might be less than truths. Noticeably, still not even calling him what he is yet. Is there a word for when irony passes satire on its way toward farce? I read a report because that's all I'm trained to do.

But we keep waking, we continue on. We proceed as if. Hopeful, if that doesn't sound too naïve. I ask Alexa for the number of deaths today and she keeps telling me what Reuters said. But I asked you, Alexa.

And it's a girl. You didn't know that, but Alexa did. She's got ideas about what we should be buying.

174 It started last night: Chilo, perpetual lap-sitter and cuddler extraordinaire, was nowhere to be found. After searching the house, we found him in my son's closet, lying in his doggy bed, which had somehow ended up there. Through the night he seemed to lose a relation to his legs. He couldn't stand. He stared off into some middle distance. Always. My wife said he was up during the night a few times, though I apparently slept through it. In the morning he was no better.

We took him to the vet first thing that morning, but only one of us could go. I google how to tell a six-year-old that he is losing his dog. Do not say you are putting him down. Do not blame it on the vet. Do not suggest he might come back. Print out this coloring book to help him deal with grief. What I really wanted to do was ask Alexa, but I didn't, because she talks too loud and we're all home always.

I print the book. Chilo got to come home for a couple hours.

TROLLING: Digital harassment. It is fine to note that this begins as fun, but with the caveat that it is only ever fun for the person who begins it. SEE ALSO: *GRIEFING*.

TRUST DEFICIT: Following.

TRUTH CONDITIONS: Semantic fun, but also a fog employed to overwhelm in the modern political context.[175]

---

175 Then there's suddenly one fewer in our small, confined new world. Perhaps we feel it more deeply than normal because there's nothing to do but sit in our house and notice it. Later that month, my cousin's kids have a bad car accident. Helicopters. Life alerts. GoFundMe. I'm close enough to those involved that I want to help, but am unsure of the process. I trust the cousin whose kids were harmed implicitly, but can't be sure who is handling the money. Then I feel bad for thinking so. Protest marches are all over the news and we argue about whether it's safe to be going. Yes, but that's the point. It's not going to be safe but that is how necessary the march is.

U

UNAPOLOGETIC: When brashness is mistaken for spine. SEE ALSO: *NO REGRETS*, where perhaps there should be.[176]

UNCONSTITUTIONAL: The most common claim heard in a falling America, normally over a small squabble with no constitutional basis.[177]

UNCOOL: People who are perceived as hot are often seen as *cool*. In such cases being uncool would be cold. Being cool is also to be chill, because it exudes confidence. In which case uncool would presumably be scalding. There are seemingly no conditions where it is cool to be lukewarm. People don't like that. Cool-headed. Hot-tempered. Chilly disposition. Cold-blooded. Hot-blooded. Icy-veined. There is, apparently, a long history of equating physical temperature to temperament.

---

176 The first time someone tells me that they never apologize because it's a sign of weakness, I think they're joking. I mean, it's not the first time I'm made aware of this attitude, of course, but I thought it an antiquated notion that died with our grandparents. It's a good friend of mine who said it, an American, while we're in Kuwait, and I am shocked that we understand this so differently. His view feels outdated, something society at large had collectively moved on from long ago. Didn't we? Did I imagine that? In this moment, he is predicting the president in a way that I was too blind to see coming.

177 Infringement seems to be the constitutional case people want to make about not wanting to stay home or wear masks, but this also casually disregards the implicit duty to our neighbors, the way natural rights necessarily get limited upon our entry into or our interaction with society.

UNDERKILL: Not when you don't kill all the way, but when you lack force to win. SEE ALSO: *OVERKILL*.

UNDERPERFORM: To do worse than expected, understudy or otherwise.

UNDERWHELM: Though common in its over/under construction, that one can simply just be whelmed was a revelation to me.[178]

---

178 My son's only interactions with other kids for most of the pandemic is over our backyard fence. He complains constantly about being bored. I'm bored, too, but want to keep him positive. If you're bored then you're boring, I say, something I heard on TV once or often. It's meant to encourage him to think creatively, but I'm not sure if it's worked.

On one side of our yard, I put out a ladder so he can yell to the kids. On the other, we have just put in a trampoline he got for his birthday, a last-minute purchase when it was clear how much time we'd be spending in the house. I can't even imagine still being in NYC through this. I Zoom with friends who are there and they confirm it's as bad as you'd think.

He plays with a boy on the other side who also has a trampoline. I see his bouncing head periodically. Sometimes I go out in the backyard because I need sunlight and I hear them. Today they are arguing about how they communicate. My son is hurt because the other kid has a tendency to leave mid-conversation and not come back. He says so, in his wonderful Boston accent. Without reply, the kid quickly disappears back into his house.

UNFALSIFIABLE: That something cannot be proven false is *not* making a statement about whether it happens to be.[179]

UNFOLLOW: Slipping out the back door of a digital friendship. The new French exit.

UNPERSON: When a person is derecognized for political or ideological reasons.

---

[179] When it's clear the economy is suffering, whatever goodwill we had is lost to the fact that people seem eager to reopen. Several governors and prominent politicians are overheard, recorded, or just say flat out—some people will have to die. Don't let the problem be worse than the cure. They say that, too. What feels so bad here is not the pragmatic approach. It's the callousness. We're not in it together, after all. Same storm. Different boats. A *Forbes* article suggests, however, that it's not that simple: the people are being *astroturfed*. It cites a report from a DNS-focused cybersecurity company concluding that the campaign to reopen seems largely centered around a lobbying group in Washington. Apparently 500 newly registered domains can all be traced back to a registered lobbyist for the state of Iowa. Here is how the article says this works:

Person with an agenda creates websites that appear like a movement other people buy into the movement because it appears to have been started by people like them. They grow the movement organically people show up at a state capital with automatic weapons, possibly with crisis actors in tow, to help solidify it.

I say it that way, but that's not really true. I'm bending backward to be fair, so we can see what the problem is without picking sides. Let's try again: GOP lobbyists are subverting democracy by registering a bunch of sites to appear as if they're homegrown—to stoke fear and hate between people—that all tie back to states' gun-rights groups. And this mountain, this seemingly insurmountable haze of hate, is just one person, perhaps helped by a few others.

As far back as 2017, the House Ethics Committee acquitted Aaron Dorr for failing to register as a lobbyist on the grounds that, in the end, he wasn't paid to be one. They suggested the loophole should be closed, as clearly he was a lobbyist, but this was not their purview. "Whether we like it or not," a local representative said, "we have to dismiss the case." Because the word *lobbying*, they say, is very vague. Had they closed the loophole, one supposes, Mr. Dorr would simply have moved into the next shadow.

A loophole is exploited, and subterfuge is the point.

UNRULY PASSENGER: Humankind on earth generally, but also flight of the anti-mask contingent. Why is it these people suddenly think they're experts on federal law? "Well, actually the FAA regulations state that . . ."[180]

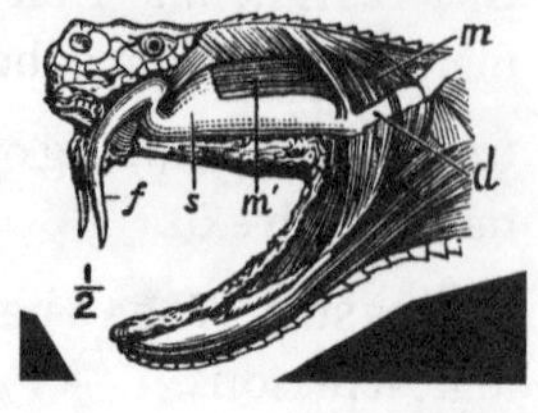

[180] In 2020, there will be 183 investigations opened into unruly passengers on planes. These numbers don't even represent the scope of the problem, as many incidents don't even get reported, partially because doing so is at the discretion of flight crew. Part of the problem, apparently, is that unruly passengers are notoriously hard to prosecute due to issues of jurisdiction. If you are in the jurisdiction of the TSA when you're in one airport, and TSA again at another, what are you when you're in the sky?

UNSAFE SEX: Sex somebody would prefer you not have, without regards to safety. SEE ALSO: *VATICAN ROULETTE*. There is, in fact, sex that is unsafe, but that is not what this is.

UNSUBSCRIBE: My friends to me, when I won't stop talking about this book.

UPLINK: That we are all satellites in a complex system. That we should mind our connections. That we must hand off between stations with great care less we degrade or drop our signals.[181]

---

[181] My neighbor, just back from an interview at John Deere because he's lost his oil industry job, asks me over the fence, mid-quarantine, if I happened to see the satellites last night. *What satellites?* I say, because I hadn't, but also because the question implied something special about them.

"Forty of 'em in a row. Just roaring through the sky. Strangest thing. They're coming again tonight. I'll send you a link."

He looks down at his phone and pushes the screen a few times. My phone beeps, but I ignore it until we're done talking about work, and money, and if there's anything we can do to help. He's one of these types who, when you offer help, he reflexively offers to help you, too, but a little more insistently. Not so much an offer as a deflection—perhaps a defense of vulnerability. I tell him I'll be sure to let him know and head back inside.

At 9:24, I manage to get Sarah to join me in the backyard. She's tired, sick from the pregnancy—all the extra hormones, she says—and is sleeping more than normal. They've doubled her hormones again since the scare. But she's interested and has stayed up to watch. These days, any change from the normal routine is welcomed as a major event. We have three minutes to walk outside and find the best spot to view the stars.

Normally, it's dark. We live in a small town on the outskirts of an only slightly bigger town, and most nights, there's little light pollution. My neighbor's left his back porch light on, a floodlight. The moon, too, seems brighter than normal. Together they obscure more than they reveal. Sarah and I walk back and forth into various corners of the yard trying to find the darkest bit. *

We're looking up, but we see nothing; a few stars here and there. Is that it? Wait. Is that it? Any set of three or more stars that look equally spaced or like a cluster of some sort is a suspect. ***

A few minutes later, from the far side of the house, Sarah spots it first. ** **

Oh, there it is. *** * * *

The confidence in her statement has me running from the other end of the backyard. Turns out, I didn't need to rush; they take several minutes to pass . . . . * . . **

. . . . in semi-regular . * . * . . patterns . . . . . . They're nothing but small twinkling lights from down here, but they don't feel like it. Their position in low orbit, and the precision with which they draw a distinct line diagonally across the sky, feels like, for the first time, the future of jetpacks and flying cars that movies promised years before. It feels like the future arriving. It doesn't even occur to me yet that they can see me, ping off the phone in my pocket. A Foucauldian notion: a panopticon in reverse, traded for the promise of a zettabyte.

Nor is it the arrival of the future, of course. That would have been the development of the internet itself more than the launching of the latest series of satellites to facilitate it. But the hubris of it shines. The grand scale of the undertaking suggests we might have a handle on this life thing, unless, of course, it's the start of something else.

UPLOAD: That what we have, inadvertently or not, downloaded, we upload elsewhere. We input. We transfer. We pass, we send, we sync. We transmit. Into our children, our relationships, our neighborhood. What is the quality of that which you are uploading?

UPMARKET: Mercurius, god of commerce, giving his sales pitch.

UPTICK: How we measure terrorist incidents, wildfires, corona cases. But you never hear of downticks. Perhaps downturn but no upturn, and turn-down service is another thing entirely. You can be turned in, turned out, turned off, turned on, perhaps turned down, if they ever turned up in the first place.[182]

---

182 This time will be known by its breakdowns. By the quickness with which America seemed to cave in under the weight of its own ideas, which had grown increasingly hollow in the name of profits. So many have chosen a version of freedom that looks petulant and small while forgetting their obligations to community. In America, the zeitgeist is such that we can't tell what our news is. What is real. There is censorship, because this president. The gift he's given is to show how fragile our systems actually are. Whatever you thought America was before, you've now been shown otherwise.

It actually takes far longer to pick apart what is not true and prove it with facts than it does for an untrue thing to carry. The Gish gallop running full speed through the great American discourse. This guy is not even a good liar, he's not even a guy you think might tell the truth, and look how quickly his bad ideas spread. This is the problem.

We are eighteen weeks and the baby is a boneless chicken breast. Sarah feels it move for the first time.

And then, four key incidents happen in the midst of an already fraught pandemic: Ahmaud Arbery, shot while black and jogging. Breonna Taylor, shot after un-uniformed cops in unmarked cars execute a no-knock warrant in the middle of the not-day. George Floyd, killed by a policeman via a sustained knee on the back of the head, while three other officers watched, after being suspected of using a fake $20 bill. And Christian Cooper, harassed for birdwatching while black. This is a microcosm of the problem: people empowered by a system that doesn't condemn their behavior; a militarized police force, increasingly antagonistic toward its citizenry, most severely against citizens of color; a white woman, who knows the power of the accusation she's making, doing so casually, because she doesn't want to leash her dog, a rule she's breaking.

And what if they weren't caught on video?

They were videoed. Caught!

What?

Wait, what? But weren't they caught on video?

[To know where that is heading is to know what the problem is.]

I recall watching both the Rodney King beating and the beating of Reginald Denny in the L.A. riots on TV, just twenty miles away. I was crying at both. If you can't take it, go in another room, my brother said.

There is not anything new or notable about this treatment, but now it is the everyday folded inside of a more traumatic time. Not even now? Not even now, when we are all collectively fighting for our lives, will you stop killing them?

UPVALUE: To overrate, underrate, pro-rate, irate.

UPWARD MOBILITY: Look at how freely they move up there ↑. Just bouncing around from one opportunity to another, from one job/love/family to another. You could too if you worked harder! Certainly no one should be judged by their station, we are where we're from; but the mental gymnastics it takes not to recognize the myriad ways each slight advantage compounds into opportunity in life can be appalling. Worse, our desire to build a narrative of our life that reinforces how we want to see ourselves can create/erase/negate some of these advantages in our own mythmaking, meaning that we don't really see each other. Or ourselves.

URBAN RENEWAL: That one's renewal is another's gentrification, imminent domain, government takeover.

USER AGREEMENT: You agreed to this—remember?[183]

UTC: Clearly the initialism for Coordinated Universal Time needs to explain itself. Somewhere, there is an American saying—*See, this is what happens when you compromise!*

---

[183] Sarah is just past eighteen weeks, and the baby is making her constantly sick. There should be a terms agreement for this, she says. We laugh imagining the minutiae of what this would entail.

UX, AKA USER EXPERIENCE: A human interpretation of a digital event, or a customer's interaction with a company, or a . . . [184]

---

[184] In July I suffer a severe back injury. Truthfully, I'm told it started a month earlier, likely when I tried out a new form for my kettle bell swing, trying to manage a freshman 15 that has morphed into a senior—seven times over now—100+ pounds. I managed to put on school weight, baby weight, and pandemic weight to spare. Something about the workout made me end abruptly at the time. I spent the month after simultaneously complaining about my back while professing that I don't actually have back problems. The pain would increase, depending on certain types of activities, then wane when I'd stop to rest. On this day, I'd been cleaning out a shed to store things that were currently in the baby's room. I'd spent a day lifting fairly heavy things, including a few old bags of cement mix left by the previous tenant, but when the injury happens, I have just tried to roll something light on wheels across the floor in an only slightly awkward position. The pain is so total that my legs start to buckle and I scream out for help to a friend who's nearby. He aids me in standing and limps me back to the house.

I spend the first few days thinking the severity of the pain will go away, the next two in and out of urgent care, then an emergency room where they seem to think I'm trying to get heavy pain killers, then my doctor's office. It's a disc hemorrhage, I'm eventually told. We're twenty-three weeks and the baby is a mango that, due to frequency but not frequency, can hear my voice but not Sarah's. All my voice is doing is announcing its pain.

I don't know yet that I'm heading for months in an office chair, in excruciating pain, unable to even get myself out of bed, or take care of my most basic needs. There will be X-rays and MRIs, emergency rooms and various shots, and extended rehab that, perhaps due to insurance, seems to end sooner than it should. As the initial overwhelming pain of the back subsides, leg pain comes in, shooting down the right leg from where the protruding disc is impinging the nerve, sciatic likely.

And time, which had already grown near meaningless in COVID days, stretched out to include the night too. For a year, I won't be able to sleep past 4 a.m., no matter how late I go to bed. Night feels like extreme and long-term jet lag. I sit in my office chair throughout many middle of the nights with clenched teeth, watching any mindless TV I can find, praying I won't need to use the restroom.

VACCINES: Give you the sickness to give you the cure. Also, a scientific blind spot wherein people who otherwise live lives guided by advances in science arbitrarily choose to believe it doesn't apply in this case.[185]

185 A vaccine is possible. They're promising one might be available soon. I still am nervous about speed to market. I don't believe it will be infested with microchips. People are already starting to say they wouldn't get it.

VAGUENESS: All this time, I thought this was a flaw that hindered communication, not a design feature that encourages it. I suppose I always thought of language development as something like a journey to a destination: that I could understand others and become better understood the more I studied, that I could eradicate ambiguity, perhaps entirely, that I could articulate emotion, the full range of it, that I could fully present my thoughts and better understand those of others. I never realized that vagueness was a built-in feature, as necessary for human interaction, perhaps, as specificity.[186]

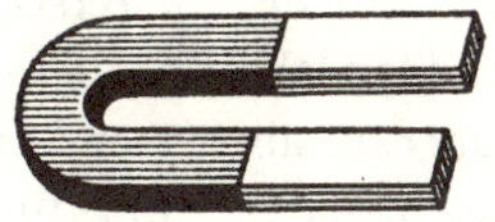

[186] A 2012 MIT study shows ambiguity makes language more efficient, partially because easily pronounced words with fewer syllables can be reused often. If every word referred to only one thing, we'd struggle to communicate any ideas of complexity. Cool, but Counterwords are another thing entirely, right?

Sarah struggles to name what she's feeling in this time, but mainly, it's sick. She wakes up so sick she doesn't know what to do with herself. Wakes up in the night sick. Runs to puke. Mortified. She doesn't want our son to think something is wrong with her so she's hiding it from him. And she's still working, on Zoom. Sometimes it gets so bad that she has to go off camera and mute while she vomits in a trash bag she keeps next to her. Nothing in particular seems to set her off—not like smells or anything, as she has heard to expect. She has thrown up so often that she cries to me that she can't do it anymore. She is worried, too, because with our son, she stopped getting sick in the second trimester. This is different, she says. Soon the doctor is also concerned because she keeps losing weight.

VANITY LABEL: A record label that is likely to make no records and is a label only in the sense that a name is a thing. Part of the late capitalism trend to invent a company, register a domain, and see if anyone shows up.[187]

---

[187] BREAKING NEWS: Neighbor's Band That You've Successfully Avoided Seeing LIVE for Months, Now Threatening to Serenade Neighborhood.

The flood of inspirational videos of quarantined people playing music for their neighbors in the midst of the ongoing response to COVID-19 continues to illustrate both the power of song to lift spirits in hard times and the communal benefits of group emoting. Musicians everywhere are reportedly seeing this as a call to action, perhaps none more so than your neighbor in that band he keeps telling you about.

Not content to sit on the sidelines and let the out-of-work philharmonic steal the spotlight, and at least a little chafed that the latest musical trend has once again started in Europe, your local bands eagerly await the chance to do their small part, and are, as of press time, tuning up and "getting show-ready."

Though you'd previously assured your neighbor that you didn't get his flyer, or that you forgot it was *that* Monday he was playing the Farmers' Market, or even that you had to *see-a-guy-about-a-thing* in the midst of their Local Music Award Season showcases, he is certain that you will not want to miss the "feel-good" feeling that his non-feel-good tracks will have when belted from his porch at the top of his lungs, particularly in light of the only recently discovered acoustic properties of the alley he lives above.

If ongoing Facebook negotiations among band members are any indicator, the show will not be without its pressures: they are fairly certain, for example, that though they likely live too far away to hear one another fully, the drummer's performance—he currently resides in a van halfway between your neighbor and the flophouse/rehearsal lockout inhabited by several other band members—will likely provide a centralized beat from which they can triangulate and stay in time.

"Not likely," according to 562couchcritic, who purports to have once heard their demo and wondered if they could hear each other even when in the same room. A sentiment that's echoed by a couple of local "sound guys" of clubs they'd previously played, who've chimed in with doubts that a "cohesive sound" is even possible "for this particular group of individuals."

Lastly, there is apparently still widespread dissent among band members themselves on exactly who the lead singer is, whether or not there will be a bass solo, and who gets to wear the iconic—but too idiosyncratic for there to be two—hat. "We simply can't be a two-fedora band," Bass-Sick69 posted to the band's page just moments ago.

An insider tip suggests that at least one band member has expressed grave concern that another free show might negatively affect their "perceived brand value," in light of ongoing negotiations with his uncle's vanity label, to which our insider responded, "Whatever, man."

But the encouragement they're otherwise receiving online by voices as disparate as a mysterious fan in Kansas, a local barista, girlfriends who are trying not to appear as such, someone named Ricci's out-of-town aunt, and at least one promoter of the Living Room Showcase Series, which is currently rebranding as the Patio Sessions, all but assure that a show will, in fact, go on at some point in the very near future.

Be wary, neighbors: showtime may come at any moment and go on for as long as they choose: gone are all semblances of third-party prequalification to take the stage; gone are any talent monitors to help predetermine the success of the show; gone are the tastemakers and gatekeepers to good music, all now archaic notions of a time likely soon to be known as pre-corona. You are indeed a captive audience and a people under siege.

VANITY PLATES: ICURN2U.

VARIABLE ANNUITY: A tax-deferred retirement vehicle, like a donated golf cart in the Caymans.

VARIABLE-RATE MORTGAGE: A gamble.

VARIANTS: Something on the horizon, happening so fast they've concluded we may need to revert to the Greek alphabet to differentiate. Not until Delta will people take variance seriously.

VATICAN ROULETTE: Unsafe sex. SEE ALSO: *THE RHYTHM METHOD*.[188]

VELVET-ROPE ECONOMY: Life commodified into tiered user experience based on monetary expenditure. This has existed since at least the *Titanic*. Et tu, Disneyland?

VICTIM BLAMING: Lawyerly sleight of hand.

---

188 When I tell my boss my back injury may prevent me from attending an upcoming meeting, he seems to not believe me, suggests I still need to attend.

I have to be driven there. I have to be helped out of the car. I limp my way inside and to the elevator. As I arrive, my boss and two counterparts are standing in front of a large lecture hall, talking. When he sees me limping in, he says, "You didn't have to come in," as if I had chosen to.

VICTIMLESS CRIME: Political sleight of hand.[189]

VIRAL, AS IN *TO GO*: Sharable, low-hanging fruit of humanity. Also, wash your hands.

---

189 A meme surfaces in the midst of the pandemic suggesting that the cart corral at your local grocery store is the best indicator as to whether or not society is going to make it. Among other things, it suggests that returning your cart when you're finished is itself objectively right, we can all do it, it is low-stakes participation in the social contract, and yet you are not required to do so by law. And many don't, because you have the right to leave it where you'd like. In the meme, cart non-returners are eventually called monsters, non-people, animals, and in that way, the meme itself does what it accuses cart non-returners of: fails to empathetically consider the other side. The pattern continues recursively.

It is easy enough to pick apart the rhetorical argument being presented: it assumes some truths that are not objectively so. It walks you down a course of logic without allowing for all sides. But that's not the point. It's funny, too, because it's an example of how preposterous and luxurious our concerns have become, global pandemic aside.

The comments cleave and fracture: *Well, I'm the kind of person that does X; My father always taught me Y; I like to punch people who do Z.* It devolves that quick. And on cue, a troll: *Yeah, I like to leave them out there just to see the look on X's and Y's faces when I do. See if I might find me a Z who wants to get at it.* Etc. Etc. Ad nauseam.

We've all been both, right? Isn't this what we all do? First we're one way, and then we're another. We look back at the older version of us embarrassedly, maybe even a little proud of our growth?

Let's say this is a hill to die on: what if I spent a lifetime just returning other people's carts for them—graciously—and never said a word about it, as an exercise of my own personal growth, as an exercise in humanity? Wouldn't that be okay, too? What if at my funeral, hundreds of people, or maybe only one, gathered and said, I'm sorry to hear he never got anywhere with that whole writing thing, but one time, he returned my cart when I was a bit rushed, saw it in my rearview as I drove away, and that always stuck with me. What if they're not actually doing it to you, but are rather, just like you, busy, sometimes a little short, maybe a little sad about the state of things? What I'm saying is maybe if I/you/we saw them last week, we'd be impressed with their growth rather than disappointed by what seemed like smallness.

VIRAL SHED: That how much you give off is commensurate with how much you have, AKA *VIRAL LOAD*.[190]

VIRTUAL: The qualifier for any number of new technologies in a digital space including, but not limited to, reality, memory, literacy, etc.[191]

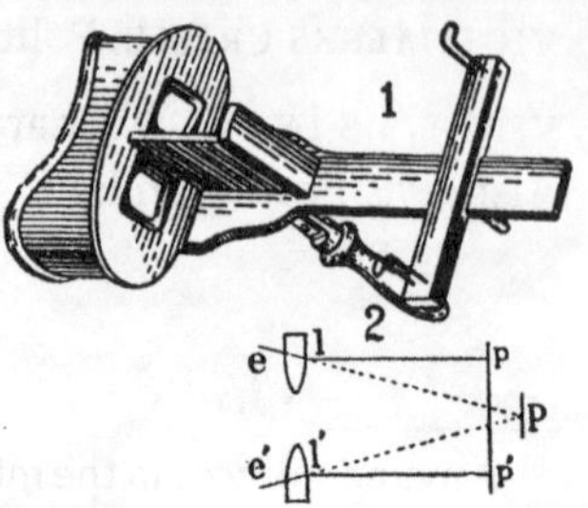

---

[190] In August, school starts for the year. I'm teaching online, a synchronous class that requires me to be on Zoom. Luckily, I'm in my office chair already and can just roll to class. I'm one of the lucky ones. In fact, I'm only allowed to teach online because I have, in addition to health concerns, a position that lets me plead my case directly to administrators. It also likely helps that I can't walk on campus even if I wanted to, though that hasn't always mattered.

But, by late in the month, I can walk out my front door and to the corner of my street, approximately fifty yards. I've saved it on my calendar, so monumental is the event. It's painful, but I can get it done. I am scheduled for physical therapy but can't get in for a couple of weeks. I decide to try a chiropractor in the meantime, even though I have concerns that it might be quackery. Truthfully, I didn't want to go but my wife said that if I don't, I can't complain about the pain. This seems reasonable. And I want to complain. I do know that some people say it's really helped them but I can't get my mother's voice out of my head; she's saying, *Once you start you can't stop with it, like it's a narcotic. They'll have to crack you all the time.*

I go, and the guy is nice enough, but it does seem, to be honest, like a bit of a sham. Everything, from his degree to his opinions on the body, to why what works does work, to watching me walk across the room so he can push me a degree or two this way or that, feels a bit shady. I go a few times, and it never stops feeling shady. But when all of this is over, when I've done everything that down-the-middle-medicine has prescribed me—save the opiates I narrowly avoided in the immediate days after—I really won't be any closer than I was here. For all of the degrees on the wall and the charts and theories, this will feel nearly if not quite as good as anything else we try. Truly.

[191] It's now West Texas–hot, Kuwait-hot even, with all days now marked in relation to the 100-degree mark. We ask Alexa about it and she seems unimpressed with our line of questioning. I can tell you other things about the weather, she says. Would you like to know the UV index? I mean, I kind of do, but I also don't want to encourage the sass.

VIRTUE SIGNALING: What good is it if you don't see me doing it?

VITAL SIGNS: Physical indicators that a person is alive without any value attributed to whether or not they are essential.[192]

---

[192] One of the distressing things, and there are many, is how empty the streets are. How silent it can be everywhere. The roads. The schools. Even here, where they're not taking it seriously at all, there is still less going on than usual. On TV, people skateboard down freeways. But in this global pause, an unexpected gift: wildlife is returning. All of our pollutions are cutting down. We accidentally meet the climate agreement requirement even though a president pulled out of it because there is no commerce. Business is a machine that needs to eat, but for now, the flora and fauna have free rein.

And Sarah keeps losing weight. At the height of the problem, late in the second trimester, she is down twenty-five pounds from her starting weight when she became pregnant. Each trip to the doctor involves the question as to whether it's better to hospitalize her or not. Soon, they say. If you don't start gaining—then we will. Soon! Always on edge. Will they or won't they? She's able to keep water down at least.

A regionally famous fast food place that specializes in milkshakes opens by our house and the nurse tells her to eat there all day every day if she can. Seriously.

We try to keep things normal at home, try to keep our son entertained with backyard activities and such. Sarah keeps needing to stop for vomit breaks. Mostly, she can pull them off without him noticing. She's still afraid of worrying him. Later, she'll say that this all made her just feel more on the periphery of things, there and not there, something beyond just isolated. And that she didn't feel like she had anyone to take care of her, because I was dealing with my own slow recovery.

VITRIOL: When I wrote for an online publisher, somewhere news adjacent but not quite, they'd A/B the headlines to see which one got more clicks. The more vitriolic would get the most attention, even if it just happened to be people telling me they thought the headline was shit. I had no defense for when this happened because the title was working as designed and it wasn't mine to begin with.

VOCAL FRY: In English, a vocal affect derided as lazy, infantile, and harmful, despite its common use in other languages, because if we can't critique your right to say anything, we'll critique how you say it. Oh, yeah—and stop destroying English.

VOICE: An author's esthetics.[193]

VOICEMAIL: The author's unavailable.

VOICE-OVER: Not talking over each other, but rather non-diegetic sound.

---

193 I teach throughout but on Zoom. And host a weekly meeting for new teachers on Zoom. And we now do Zoom calls, too, to say hi to various people, though it's always uncomfortable. We just want to hear someone else's voice. Sometimes, we also want to see their face. Sometimes, we then regret having wanted to see their face as we all seem to be falling apart in isolation. My hair grows to a length midway down my back, the longest it's been in my life, and I'm the only one who seems to think it looks at all good. We Zoom with friends in New York City and California, nine of us. All of the friends in New York either have COVID at the time of the call or will soon. All work in food service. I see family on Zoom and we game on Zoom and remember when *zoom zoom* was about going and evoked the idea of leaving, of speed, of being in motion, but now it's only stagnant, Zoom is the language of clipped opportunity, of house arrest, of isolation and simulated real-time non-personal group connection. This buffering, clipped, is that you or is it me, robotic-tinged tonal approximation of connection is wildly insufficient, but we are so isolated that we crave it. Long for it. Schedule it. Can't wait for it to come because at least it's something. It's not much but it's something. Please give me some sort of something in this.

VOMITORIUM: A part of the Coliseum in Rome where people would go to vomit or have sex, or both, as they were moved by the violence occurring inside.[194]

VOTER SUPPRESSION: A systemic attempt to keep people from the poll.

---

[194] This is according to a guide at the Coliseum itself several years back. He described it as personal preference, as a kink or fetish, a *whatever you're into* sort of thing. But I find out years later that maybe that's not the case at all. That although *vomitoria* does stem from a word meaning "to spew forth," the actual meaning is an entry or exit for large amounts of people to go through at once. When viewed from a distance it could actually appear like the building was spewing forth people. And while I suppose this doesn't alone contradict the possibility that people could have still had sex and/or vomited there, it does mean the loss of the bacchanalian suggestion that people were in equal parts repulsed and aroused by the sight of blood and gore, of death. Have I been spreading misinformation all this time? Should I have sought out a better authority—could there have been one?—than a tour guide at the place where it was said to have happened? Or is this just a misunderstanding on either his or my part? Something approximating truth, lost in the telephone game of time.

Sarah's sickness continues throughout the second trimester. Much worse than last time, she says. Because I am largely confined to a chair and need her help for most things, she often vomits near me. So great is my body weight, compared to hers, that the stress of having to lift me causes her to vomit. Not solely from the effort, of course. Still, it's hard not to feel like it's my fault. I also feel repulsive.

There is a sliding scale now between my improvement and her increased incapacity to move. Something falls on the ground in between us, say, and we stare each other, as if to say, who gets to hurt this time? In the beginning, the back is bad enough that it's usually her. Soon though, there is increasing risk to her straining to lift anything and we switch.

WAR ON DRUGS: A marketing strategy.

WARP SPEED, OPERATION: Because nothing engenders safety like bragging about speed to market.[195]

WASH YOUR HANDS: A plea, and our primary line of defense.[196]

WAVE: Peaks and valleys. Repeat. How many waves are needed to make a set? I want to collect them all.

WEASEL WORDS: When words wield wiggle room the weasel is working his way.

---

[195] When a vaccine does finally come, a president will claim a victory that's not his. Credit really goes to an mRNA tech or the company that the tech worked for, or the two German immigrants who invented the technology. Also, he's convinced his followers to see no contradiction in praising him for it, while at the same not believing it does enough to warrant taking it. This should be his legacy.

Here's the thing, though: he didn't even come up with the flashy name of the operation himself. He copied it. Stole it. It was originally dubbed "Project Lightspeed" by German company BioNTech, owned by the two scientists who invented mRNA technology, Dr. Ugur Sahin and Dr. Özlem Türeci. A president stays true to his track record: steals someone else's ideas and claims them as his own. Grift.

[196] A friendly reminder that it is likely time to do so again. And quit touching your face.

WE DON'T KNOW WHAT WE DON'T KNOW: About a presidency, about a virus, about the coming months and years and this great division that keeps us from seeing each other. But we know that's what it is. That there is divisiveness. That it's being fostered as a strategy. That it's building to something.[197]

WHATABOUTISM: Counteraccusation as a pivoting strategy. AKA *WHATABOUTERY* or the *WHATABOUTS*, not to be confused with the *WHOSEITFOR'S* or the *THAT'S-A-FINE-HOWDOYOUDO'S*.

WHATCHAMACALLIT: A word in wait for the word you mean; a placeholder. *AKA CHINGADERA, DOOHICKEY*, or *THINGAMAJIG*.

---

[197] Late September, I nearly get it myself, by leaving home to help a friend who has a flat tire on the freeway but doesn't have the right jack. I can't change a tire myself as I can still barely walk, can't bend down, but I have a jack, so I go. Lifting the jack itself is hard. Getting into my car is difficult, the first time I've driven anywhere but a hospital in nearly two months. I hop in my car to help her with the tire, along with another friend who arrived before I did. I have the jack; he can do the work. Though outside, it is the closest I've been to other people in months. She texts the two of us the next morning and says she's tested positive.

We're at twenty-eight weeks, the start of the third trimester, and the baby is an eggplant. We rush to get tested for COVID. Sarah is mad at me. Rightfully, it feels like, because I have risked our own family's precarious health by trying to help someone else. This line, to me, is trouble. That I can't just help someone who might need it. That scares me.

The friend has been, she claims, safe. Which then becomes mostly safe, but when she says where she's actually been going, I realize that we have different definitions of safe in the current climate. What stings most is that I feel I now need to be suspicious of my intent to help others. That help, too, can be dangerous. That this instinct has caused me to put my family in danger. That is a thought I'm not entirely ready to process.

We work with our son to manage expectations about Halloween. The neighbor a block over puts up a pirate ship so big that people come to our neighborhood from across the city to see it. We hide indoors, distressing over whether it's morally right to even leave a bowl of candy outside. After the holiday the number of cases skyrockets and the hospitals become swarmed, as people have long feared.

WHAT HAPPENS IN VEGAS, STAYS IN VEGAS *(PHRASE)*: A geographical phenomenon cum sales pitch for a city, where unique and unknown metaphysical properties within the municipal boundaries are such that any activities that occur within its 135.86 square miles are forgotten upon departure, a memory loophole particularly exploited by those prone to engage in vices of all manner.

WHISTLEBLOWER: Not the blowing of whistles.[198]

---

[198] In a blog post titled "Bye, Amazon," a VP for the company announces his resignation after the corporation fires whistleblowers who were making noise about warehouse employees' fears of exposure to the virus. He links to an over-nine-hour video of Amazon employees speaking against the corporation that I've otherwise never heard on the news. The video has fewer hits than your average cat video.

At an hour and fourteen minutes in, they decide to restart from the top after technical difficulties, and you can almost hear a boardroom in Seattle breathe a sigh of relief. Nothing to worry about here because they don't seem professional. But they do, technical difficulties aside. They so clearly know what they're talking about and seem to want to help. They are earnest, knowledgeable. Invested. Then one person interrupts the restart because people did, in fact, hear the intros. This is not about perfection, she says. Clearly. But this is part of the trouble. Present-day lies are glossy. Produced. Managed. The truth—the small person trying to break through—is unpolished, unproduced, sometimes even haphazard, and subsequently fights an uphill battle. This, too, will matter.

WHITE-COLLAR CRIME: A bias used to justify disproportional sentencing. Blue-collar crime is siding with the bosses against your coworkers.

WHITE FLIGHT: Karen, in a rush to speak with your manager.

WHITE NOISE: Everything pushed into the background of non-consideration. Bias. Trauma. The concerns of your neighbor. The long list of tasks to complete. The news when you're inundated and overwhelming you is the point.[199]

WHITE-TRASH COBBLER: I've strained myself trying to rename this, but Anglo-poverty cobbler has no stickiness to it and sounds *more*, rather than less, problematic.[200]

WHITEWASH: To cover up and conceal.

---

[199] My mother, who works in the hotel industry, has her wage reduced 25 percent, then her work reduced to half-time, all while finishing a home remodel she now can't afford. My cousin in the sports industry loses his job but is offered freelance work. My friends who are waiters in New York both got COVID-19, and we realized that four out of eight on our latest Zoom call are likely infected. My friend who works in a California restaurant, who used to hide from a warrant in NYC, was laid off but should wait around because they may reopen soon. My other friend in commercial work has no jobs to speak of. My friend who was starting a business has stalled in the water and his wife has decided on divorce. My old boss in Kuwait praises the Gulf nation governments for how they've handled the virus but only in ways that work in jabs at America when he does.

[200] Place one bag of frozen peaches in a baking dish. Pour one box of dry yellow cake mix over the top. Pour one can of cream soda over the top of that. Bake until golden. Seriously.

WILLFUL BLINDNESS: Avoiding the truth at all costs.[201] Because I'm in America at present, there is almost no pandemic conversation that isn't an economic conversation.

WITH ALL DUE RESPECT *(PHRASE)*: As a prepositional phrase, a sign that none is coming.[202]

WMD: We were promised yellowcake. Uranium, of course, but yellowcake nonetheless.

WOKE: Do you think during the Enlightenment there were people using it as an accusation? *Look how REASONED these people are acting—the worst!*

WRINGER: To be put through. Zaps all of your energy.[203]

WTF: Whiskey Tango Foxtrot, or an inquiry as to what is the actual fuck.

---

201 Some rhetoric is more transparent than others.

202 A passenger on a Delta flight from Miami to Atlanta slaps the flight attendant for asking her to put her mask back on. On an easyJet flight from Belfast to Edinburgh, a woman is arrested for refusing to wear a mask and shouting "Everybody dies" on the plane. A woman attempting to travel from Nashville to Las Vegas is kicked off a flight before departure, forcing the entire plane to deboard. As passengers air their grievances about the inconvenience she's caused everyone else, missed connections and such, she keeps yelling, "I'm allowed. I'm allowed."

203 I have initiative.

NOT AT ALL SLIGHTLY SOMEWHAT A LOT

WWW: A seemingly inert creation that would come to destroy the world.[204]

[204] When I mention this project, one that is ostensibly about language but at some point gets taken over by the coronavirus, a professor tells me that at the time the internet started, some people suggested that WWW actually stood for 666, suggesting that the arrival of the devil is the new technology and predicting Christ's second coming. A byproduct of a true paradigm shift, perhaps, like the invention of the printing press. Have we always loved conspiracy theories? Is this just a sign of the anxiety new technology prompts? So common is the attribution of the number 666 to some current anxiety that it is actually hard to research. Is it the devil's number on an energy drink? Is it the sign of the United Nations? Is it maliciously hidden within our barcode systems? It's a symbol that travels well. All of which leads to a new term indicating fear of the number: *hexakosioihexekontahexaphobia*. Is there a word, though, for fear of excessively long words?

XANTHAN GUM: A thickening agent found in glue and salad dressings. Also used for dysphagia patients when things become too hard to swallow . . . [205]

XENAGOGY: Has this inadvertently become a guidebook for a pandemic?

XENIAL: Hospitality between host and guest, from the ancient Greek. How you should host somebody.

205 Something hard to swallow: a neighbor two houses down passes away, a COVID death, though it is unclear if it will be counted as such. After his wife got it and was turned away from a local hospital due to capacity, forced to deal on her own, he responded likewise when he got it. When he is rushed to the hospital for liver failure after taking too much Tylenol to reduce his fever, they still don't have room. They airlift him to a hospital in San Antonio. When it looks bad, the grandparents make the ten-hour drive with the kids to say goodbye, but he's gone before they arrive. That fast. We're thirty weeks, but it feels uncouth to mention it here, near so much tragedy, ongoing.

Our other neighbor sets up his pirate ship in the front yard, and kids from all over the city come to trick or treat. Most years it feels like a gift he is giving the neighborhood. That's how he sees it too, he says. This year it feels like something else. We decide to set out a bowl of candy after all. The baby is a zucchini.

XENOGLOSSY: To speak a language one has never learned.[206]

XENOPHOBIA: For as long as I can recall, I've wished people would just be honest about their prejudices. I figured I'd respect them more. We know you feel this way. Don't be a coward, I'd think. Say it. But now I think this was misguided. Now I see this as a position fostered by a system that at least pretends to outwardly condemn xenophobia, racism, and all forms of prejudice as wrong. Since the racists have surfaced, emboldened by a government making room for them, winking their racism into acceptance, I want nothing more than for them to crawl back into their hole.

---

[206] One of the things that seems most apparent is that we're no longer all speaking the same language. Or we're saying the same words but hearing different things in them, perhaps. So many words, in this book or otherwise, are sending us down different courses; they index political positionality in ways we are triggered to respond to. It is September and a president won't commit to a peaceful transfer of power. We'll have to wait and see, he says. He's praising the job he's done in his handling of the currently out-of-control pandemic. It is all so absurd on its face that I would fall on the floor laughing were it not for the fact that, turning to each side of me, I see others agreeing with him. I try to remind myself how tantalizing it is to be sold the things we want to hear. That the people whom he is most manipulating are those who are following him. I first feel bad for how duped they will feel when they figure it out, then realize that they probably think the same about me. But the difference between arguing false equivalence and simply believing you're right is lost in the current moment.

XERIC: Life on the Llano Estacado.[207]

XERISCAPE: My wildest dreams for my current front yard.

XEROCHILIA: Send lip balm now, please.

XL: One person's extra large is another's slim fit. Or doesn't fit, admittedly.

---

[207] By September we're all back in school at full force. I'm in physical therapy. A doctor tells me that 50 percent of the time a person with my injury recovers 90 percent of mobility. I struggle to do the math while trying to balance on one foot pulling an oversized rubber band. Two to three times per week I go to a side room at the local gym. I learn to roll a ball in front of me. I try to catch a ball. Someone stretches my leg to one side and then the other.

The rules require us all to mask up but one guy refuses to. He talks a little too loud, gets a little too in my space, flaunts the mask rules so spectacularly I'm shocked nobody says anything. I suggest to the personnel, after several weeks of this, that I'd appreciate not being scheduled when he's present or I'm going to have to say something to him. I feel petty for doing so. They pretend to appreciate my comment. Soon after, they say I'm ready for traction and start putting me on a device that most closely resembles a medieval rack. I hope these last two events are not related.

In the machine, your upper half is strapped in a fixed position, while your waist is strapped on a sliding track for movement. The entire point of the machine is to pull the lower half of your body from the upper half, which is fine so long as it's not set too high. It hurts and it feels good; for a little while the nerve isn't being pinched. Then the pain returns.

An ex-coworker figures that if COVID hasn't infected her husband who works at a prison, then maybe it's not that serious. My friends who do or do not work for the federal government are mum about what is or isn't happening. My stepfather, hiding in the desert, doesn't believe me when I say we're good and sends me a gallon-sized bottle of isopropyl alcohol from some inside guy he's got somewhere. My brother was going to have to take a pay cut until my mom told him to tell his boss that it is illegal to pay him any less. They respond, Oh, I guess you're right, a week later. Meanwhile, her own pay remains diminished.

XO: Kisses first, then hugs, but for now, airkisses and airhugs, from a distance.[208]

XXL: Extra, extra-large and my current shirt size.[209]

XXX: A thirty in Rome, a turkey in bowling, a warning in film.

---

[208] My mother-in-law is Zooming a lot more because she is all alone and feeling the strain of it. My neighbor has lost his job. My cousin keeps posting conspiracy theories on the internet, and maybe he doesn't know he's the demographic for it: middle-aged, white, lower socioeconomic and educational status, aggrieved. My brother who does bomb disposal on military bases is essential but not enjoying it. My student is in the National Guard and is just gone from class one day when he gets called up. Then he's back. Then he's gone again. My other student is also just gone from class one day and might have COVID and is hospitalized for an extended stay. I never see him again. Ever. My student who works in a care home is the last to be tested and is awaiting results. My son is now planning everything in the context of "when people are not sick, can we . . ." and it's a hard frame to hear because I don't know when that time is. Some future time, undefined. And when anyone asks, I just say, because it's mainly true, we're fine, pretty much, just locked down tight. Taking it seriously is all.

[209] Subtract one X from above for when this book started and add an X to above by the time it's finished.

Y'ALL: Because even the phrase "you guys" has an inside and outside to it.

Y'ALL QAEDA (AKA *VANILLA ISIS*): I know this is supposed to be a joke, but it's more like an optical illusion. What is absurd on its face becomes truer when viewed in earnest.

YELLOW: A premonition of fall, a sign a baby is jaundiced or an adult is bottled.

YELLOWBELLIED SAPSUCKER: A hummingbird, brave or otherwise.

YELLOWBELLY: A coward.

YELLOWCAKE: The tastiest of all Urania, though most commonly now brown or black.

YELLOW-DOG CONTRACT: An employment contract wherein a prospective worker, if he wants to be a worker, promises not to be an organized one.

YELLOW JOURNALISM: Based on sensationalism, crudeness, and eye-catching headlines to help facilitate ad sales.[210]

[210] "Amazon VP Quits over 'Chickenshit' Firing of Whistleblowers." "Amazon VP Quits over 'Chickenshit' Firing of Workers." "Amazon VP Slams the 'Chickenshit' Management." "Amazon VP Resigns, Calls Company Chickenshit." Etc., etc., etc.

YELLOW PAGES: Once your only guide to the immediate world around you. All places and people reachable by a telephone. Now, just an idea older people sometimes reference, like—I'm told—when a whole neighborhood shared one phone line.[211]

YEOMAN: Your assistant.

YIELD TO MATURITY: That some of us take longer to mature than others. That there is an equation to determine if it's worth it for the investor. That you must quantify your potential for return.[212]

---

211 In most jurisdictions, a party line had a legally binding requirement that you had to hang up to let someone else use the phone in a case of emergency. I laugh at how clearly this would not work today. I want to see this as one more way in which our technological advancements have eroded our feelings of interconnectedness, and it has, but then I also learn that in Rhinebeck, New York, in 1955, a woman was indicted by a grand jury for refusing to get off the phone so people could call the fire department about a grass fire. Or, in June 1970, a sixteen-year-old girl and a woman were charged for not relinquishing the line to allow for a distress call as three boys drowned in a pond in Walsenburg, Colorado. This is, in fact, who we've always been, but that doesn't mean it's not getting worse.

212 The baby is breech. The doctor suggests we just have to wait and see what happens, but before she leaves, a nurse shares some tricks to encourage the baby to flip. Old Wives' Tales, apparently, and it's all I can do to not rush to add that to this dictionary when she says so. For starters, place ice on your stomach. We're gonna freeze her out. The cold on your belly will cause the baby to flip. Try it. Try it again. When that doesn't work, pivot. Have you tried swimming? Never mind that the ever-growing amount of swelling in your legs makes your bottom half look as if it belongs to someone other than the owner of your top half, you must get in the pool, despite the ogling eyes of the old men staring. Here's the good part—do handstands in the pool. You want to convince the baby that down is up and up is down and she should flip. Be a good host. Eventually, we will find that it doesn't matter—the baby is too large to flip.

YIN AND YANG: That your opposition might be more connected to you than you think.[213]

YIPE: A yelp.

YIPPEE: A yipe.

YOLO: You only live once, apparently.[214]

YOU KNOW WHAT I MEAN: A conversational check-in, not actually asking.

YUCKY: So many things, actually. But also a sign that I have grown overwhelmed enough to wish to retreat from the serious business of words by reverting to a childlike reaction.

YUPPIE: Young urban professional, but when they grow up, a boomer.[215]

---

213 My son seems to be getting overly emotional, but I can't say if it is just because he is spending more time with us, or if we are being different with him because we are spending more time with him. Still, he cries at the slightest correction. The hardest thing for him in this time is the isolation. Because we live in between two houses with multiple children—four on one side, five on the other—he constantly hears kids at play. Still, he has a yard to play in, which is more than he had just three years ago.

This too is an anxiety: that you have no right to feel bored when other people are dying. It's unequivocally true, so then you feel depressed and bored. Alive. Depressed. Scared. Bored.

If you're bored, you're boring, my son now says to me often.

214 A new modest proposal: the Americans for Living in Another Person's Shoes Act, aka the Love Thy Neighbor Act. All people have to move every two-three years, the primary purpose being to put blue people in red states and vice versa. Don't get too comfortable. Keep changing your friend base. It is harder to hate your neighbor than it is someone in another state. Or something like that. I know this is a solution to a problem that doesn't exist, or rather, doesn't focus on what the problem actually is.

215 Our house of stuff is still out there. Since we've moved to Texas we've been talking about having it delivered. We likely don't have the room. And we know we're not staying here, so what's the point? Perhaps at our next stop.

Z

ZEITGEIST: A new march toward oblivion.[216]

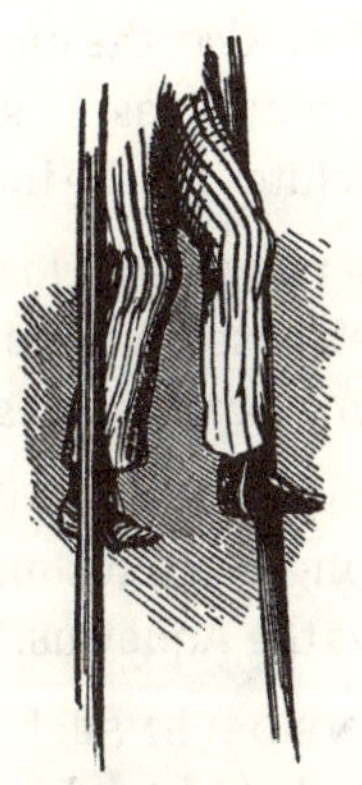

[216] When an election happens, it transpires almost exactly as expected, which is not to say that anyone knew who would win. Prognosticators don't even want to guess at a winner, given how wrong they'd all been in the previous election. But the early voting totals versus the mail-in totals is the thing. Early on in the night, the numbers in key states favored one candidate, and as the night wore on they flipped.

Speaking of flipping: the baby shows no sign of wanting to move. Sarah is beginning to swell in the legs, first minor, then more severe. Edema. What starts in the foot is soon up to the knees. She is due in three weeks. We arrange for Sarah's mother to come to us again, but just to the house this time, because there are strict rules at the hospital of how many people can come: one.

She agrees to, happily.

ZERODAY: Perhaps it doesn't always pay to be vulnerable.

ZERO-SUM GAME: In game theory, politics, and at the supermarket, one person's gain means another person's loss. As a bias, zero-sum thinking suggests . . . winners and losers. Winners. Losers.

ZERO-TOLERANCE POLICY: An escalation, the security equivalent of don't make me tell you again.[217]

ZETTABYTE: A multiple of the unit byte, to the seventh power, best currently conceived as either 1 million terabytes or 1 trillion gigabytes. Also, the monthly data-flow capabilities currently promised by companies pursuing a constellation system of low earth orbit satellites for the internet.

ZIP CODE: The closest we will come to predicting the future. Or a life's possibilities predicted, because where you live is an index of a myriad of variables.

ZODIAC: The best way to determine if two humans are capable of a long-term, sustained coupling is to look up at the stars and ask, says the Aquarius. Those are satellites, replies the Virgo.

ZONE DEFENSE: In sport, the move from man-to-man coverage to one that instead protects physical space.[218]

217 The new policy on unruly passengers on airplanes. Buy stock in duct tape.

218 In the last week, the swelling has risen as high as the waist. Between the water retention and the pressure all this puts on the uterus, they decide that a C-section is the only way. Sarah's mom has to bump up her trip by a week because there is worry we may need to go to the hospital sooner.

ZONE OF COMBAT: A designation of physical space and a tax exclusion for foreign-earned income.

ZONE OF SILENCE: A particular spot where frequencies align such that you can't hear something when standing in a certain spot, though it can be heard both nearer and farther.[219]

---

219 We can't hear each other anymore. This is evident. I don't know much, but I know we need to. One thing a peripatetic life can do, if you choose, is to give you empathy for many types of living. Reading and writing can do that too, I've found. This is because they demystify the other, make them real. Make them, if you choose it, friends. To see the similarities between Kuwait City and Lubbock, Texas, is to know a little secret about the world, to see the same smile on the face of my Egyptian boss at a magazine in the Middle East and a corporate boss in the States, between a neighbor at John Deere and good friends who are working in restaurants in NYC. This is to melt time, to diminish space. To suddenly exist in a world where they can all be shuffled interchangeably in a material way: I wake up, I engage with one, then another—through social media, through Zoom—regardless of borders and international territories, all confined to the same temporary sentence, all trying to find a way through, all balancing our families and our hopes and our need to simply step outside and maybe hug each other, to feel the relief of communion. Our communal need for each other is a secret too. It's a secret we are trying to suppress, maybe, most days, because to articulate that we aren't whole without each other is also a small truth, a hidden truth. But oh, when we get out again, what an embrace it will be!

ZOOM FATIGUE: There is a reason you feel more tired despite having done little. It is the body's emotional response to working overtime to read the social signals of fifteen people at a time. SEE ALSO: *ZOOMBOMBING; ZOOM FUNERAL, AKA THE ZOOMERAL;* and *ZOOMERAL ETIQUETTE.*[220]

---

[220] Late in the year, I attend a Zoom funeral for my grandfather Roberto, a COVID death, though it is unclear if it will be counted as such, old as he is, complications as he has. There is confusion over the link, whether it's been sent to the grandkids or not. There is confusion, too, as to whether or not the family slideshow at the beginning counts as a pre-show or the main event. As it approaches, I will ask if it starts in half an hour, and my brother will say that it's already started. None of us are good at this.

I log in just in time to see a few pictures of us kids with our grandfather that I haven't seen in years, a few that I never knew existed. 246 people will log in for it, so important is he to his small Southwest community.

He was an elder in the local church, where he'd led a Spanish-language congregation for the past twenty-five years. The funeral is primarily in Spanish, which neither my siblings nor I speak well. We will fail to understand our grandfather's funeral, at least in part. We will text back and forth instead, making fun of each other's COVID haircuts, the strangeness of seeing each other dressed up. I wonder who's wearing shorts. I am.

ZOONOTIC: A disease normally found in animals that is transferred to humans, and how this pandemic business is said to have started to begin with. We can't even agree on that.[221]

[221] I have motivation:

NOT AT ALL | SLIGHTLY | SOMEWHAT | A LOT

ZOON POLITIKON: That we are animals who need each other to survive. That as one elder goes away a new one is created. That a herd expands and contracts, and we have our roles. That I was there this time, when my child was born. That we arrived in the middle of the night to an eerily empty hospital. That I took so many pictures you'd think I was making up for something. And that before you know it, she was just there. Healthy. Crying. Our one, determined little egg, now staring at me quizzically.[222]

---

222 The first time it happens, we're all sleeping. I'm wakened by a song, a saccharine pop/rock tune, coming from somewhere just outside of our hospital room. It's tinny, likely from a phone, a ringtone perhaps. I wait for someone to answer it, but they don't. It's the middle of the night, I think, though in the fluid state of life with a newborn, time grows meaningless. Stretches. Dissolves. In the midst of the pandemic it's amplified—not just hours that we're missing, but whole calendar days. Months. When is it, exactly? It's dark, but not as dark as it will get.

I'm paused in dreaded anticipation of either new baby or Mama waking. Nurses come in once every hour or so to check their stats. There's concern. I tiptoe to the door to ask whomever to turn it down, but when I get there, both song and stranger are gone. The halls—like the freeway, the malls, the restaurants—are empty. The delivery itself was the largest gathering we'd attended in months.

Recently, someone's been letting their dog shit on my lawn. It's not a big deal, until it is. It's one thing, I rationalize—to my partner, neighbors—to not bring a bag on a walk one day, it's another to become someone's personal porta potty. Isn't it? While in the throes of this great tragedy, a meme coincidentally surfaces speculating that the cart corral at the grocery story is the best indicator of the health of a communal society. My agreement is self-righteous. So many of us are sick.

The next time the song plays, we're all awake. It's midday. It's funny. I can hear the lyrics this time: *This will be the best day of my li-i-ife.* It's not a song we'd listen to but is somehow one we know. Ear worm. Full-bodied, I imitate the staccato and rhythmic, repeating /aɪ/ sound that serves as the song's following line. Sarah laughs. But when the song plays again an hour later, it elicits a disapproving head shake. *Some people.* We begin to speculate on its origin. We blame a mystery nurse—it must be a nurse, we've determined by now, or they'd have left already—walking around pestering the entire ward with their sonic debris.

By the second time on the second day, we've elevated it to eye-roll status. We try and fail to ignore it.

Later that night, I wake to a baby's screams and Sarah trying to get out of bed to complain to whomever that the song woke them. Both body and baby are weights she should not be lifting. It grates, is all, and then it's more: intrusion, or something approaching it. The inconsideration. It's just so rude.

For two more days health steadily improves, but the song does not. We argue about whether we should say something or let it go. We take turns, over time, on who is taking which position. It all feels so petty. There is beauty, here, too, but this is not that story.

In the wee hours of our last day, the song plays shortly before a new nurse enters our room. We think we've found her, the mystery nurse revealed, but deflate when it becomes clear that it's playing from somewhere beyond her. Perhaps sensing our overwhelming angst or what is surely by now a Pavlovian twitch, she turns to us before leaving. *Oh, y'all hear that? Isn't it wonderful?*

Of all the words, this one baffles. How's that? I ask. *Didn't nobody tell y'all?* she asks, hands on hips. *The COVID ward is right above you.* My face must read: doesn't get it. After a pause she continues.

Every time a patient gets well enough to be released, all the nurses and doctors line up in the halls and cheer for them as they're escorted out. Sarah and I can't even look at each other.

Isn't it just the most touching thing?

It truly is, I say, so small I want to crawl inside myself.

We're discharged not long after. The hospital is a ghost town as we leave. Hall after hall void of people. Occasionally, we glimpse a passing nurse, floating silently between doorways. We drive home on an empty freeway, unable to unhear the song's melody. Unable to unknow its new meaning. I search the radio, certain it must be playing somewhere, craving connection. Nothing. It's dark, but not as dark as it will get.

ZUGZWANG: What life in these days feels like.[223]

ZYZOGETON: A leafhopper, and the last word in the English language.

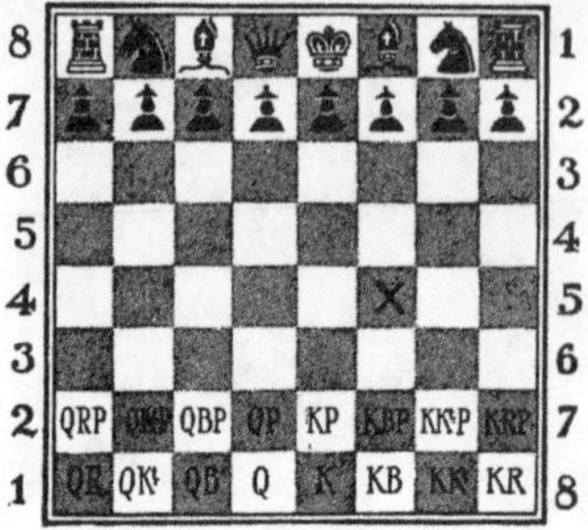

[223] We pull into the driveway, excited to see our son after three days away, the longest of his young life. We're eager to introduce him to his new sister. We get out of the car, careful with the new bundle. We're careful with Sarah, too, who's still healing. And she meets her brother for the first time and it's nice to feel a growth, an expansion, amid so much contraction. Amid the grandfather gone and the neighbor gone and the dead dog gone and the family she won't meet for a couple of years still and this terrible degree that will guarantee no job but is if nothing else terminal and the ongoing health issues and the friends in trouble and the country on fire—but we're breathing out here and this tiny life a new tiny bundle of possibilities and what will we do what future will we leave for you nothing maybe I have nothing yet but I can start small in this house with these neighbors on this block and build outward for you I can build you something small of your own I can write you words I can give you a story that is bigger and better than my story I can cut and paste the past I can alt+delete problematic family and family patterns, I can try and start something new and maybe when I'm gone, which I hope won't be as soon as it has felt lately, and there are so many reasons to be unsure, but maybe when I'm gone you'll see this story and know that you were loved wholly, the both of you, that there were parents, albeit flawed, who once were brave enough to try and bring you forward even amid all the unknowing because we have love and love is not nothing love is something love is in the bleed love is in these hands and in all of the things we build, including books. It's winter here. It's winter now. The winter they've been warning of is here. But it's no big deal. I don't want you to worry or think it's a big deal. I assure you, kiddo, it's no big deal, see, we're just gonna hole up in this little cave and wait it out. We're gonna ride it out. We're gonna just silently grow in this little pocket and stay vigilant and hope for the best. Don't worry.

ZYZYXIA: A Central American cousin of the sunflower, Zyzyxia lundellii.[224]

ZYZZYVA: A snout-nosed beetle and another last word in the English language.[225]

[224] Around 1990, when botanist John L. Strother revises the North American genera of the subtribe Ecliptinae in the sunflower family for *Systematic Botany Monographs*, he notices that some of the genus Wedelia look markedly different before concluding that this must be a new and previously unnamed genus of plant. Unfortunately, the lengthy manuscript is already in the proof stage, and the publisher refuses to incur the costly changes that would be required to add the new genus. Strother solves this by simply naming it the last word to appear on the alphabetical list.

[225] Because I'm getting conflicting answers, I ask Alexa, for fun: Alexa, what is the last word in the English language? She replies in her robotic monotone, "Hmm, I don't understand. Try something like, how do you say hello in Spanish." What has she been hearing lately to make her respond so?

ZYZZYX: The word a salesman made up to hawk fizzy seltzer as medicinal aid out in the Mojave Desert. Said he wanted his to be *the last word on medicine*; now a road in the American Southwest.[226] I can't help but think of these men together, Curtis H. Springer, a president, my father. They reflect and refract off each other. The through line is hubris, the through line is selfishness. The through line is the people in their wake. There is something particularly American about them.

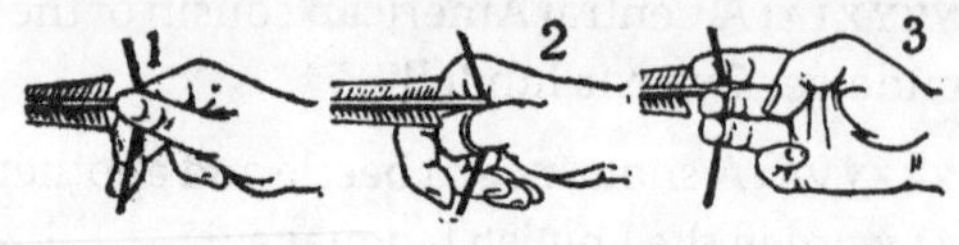

ZYZZYZUS: A marine tubulariid, and also another last word that eventually isn't.

---

[226] On December 31, word has gotten out about our planned pan-banging New Year's Eve celebration. The neighbors want in. Since this is an outside event, it seems okay. Our son needs to play with his friends, we rationalize. At midnight, some fifteen kids gather in the driveway of our neighbor's house to all bang pots and pans together. The scene is chaotic. It's a frigid evening, and the kids run as much for heat as from excitement. Though we are three families living in a row, the kids have not been together like this in a year now. We are minus one in this group, though nobody says it out loud. Matt was his name, and he's gone. One in three has lost their father. One in three has lost her husband. Still, it's hard to not feel celebratory with them, even knowing a deep underlying grief is here too. It's good—truly good—to see them, and to be seen. But we're the only ones wearing masks, and we try to keep some distance. The kids are ecstatic to be doing something that feels naughty: making noise, making their presence known in the night when they should be sleeping.

But we cause a ruckus. We scream and we bang pans and the kids run around like wild animals. A few neighbors without children peer out, wondering what we're up to. We're out here, world, banging these pots and pans together to let you know we're alive. To ward any spirits off, whether or not we believe in them. To celebrate making it through another year. We're mostly all here and we're mostly all celebrating this moment, however brief.

ZZYZER: Any word added to the end of the English language for purposes that exist outside of semantical, lexicographic, or grammatical purposes, normally commercial in nature.[227]

[227] I am sending these dispatches to you from within the pandemic, year one, second wave, GMT-5. It is silent where I am, and we are doing okay so far.

Acknowledgments

This book would not have been possible without the care, time, and help of a few people. Thank you to Johnny Carrera, who, through a fortuitous mutual acquaintance, I was able to reach out to regarding images. His lending the rights to these—particularly during Covid, when I would not have had access to the archives where the original woodblocks are—proved pivotal. This meeting, about halfway through the project, changed and enlarged what I thought this could be. Thanks also to Dr. Curtis Bauer for making that introduction and who worked with me on other projects around this text and time. To Dr. Jill Patterson, who guided me through some of the earliest iterations of the text and helped expand my understanding of forms. Thank you to Writing by Writers (and the wonderful cohort of writers I met there) for the support of a residency while I worked on this project. To Jacob M. Hall, my PhD cohort buddy and one of the earliest readers of this text, always with a keen eye and meaningful feedback. And to my family, near and far, thank you for all your support.

This book contains previously published material reprinted with permission.

"The Difference Little" (page 23) originally appeared on Pidgeonholes (2019), https://pidgeonholes.com/2019/07/the-difference-little/.

"A Case Is a Wave" (page 26) was published in *The Roadrunner Review* 7 (Spring 2021).

"The Night That Nothing Happened" (page 48) was published on Wanderlust (2021), https://wanderlust-journal.com/2021/10/16/the-night-that-nothing-happened/.